Contents

Series preface		4
London in the 1980s		5
1 People		7
Population change		7
Age and sex structure		9
Population density		11
Socio-economic groups		12
Ethnic groups		15
Inner city aid		18
Crime		20
2 Housing		21
Housing problems		21
Housing tenure		25
Thamesmead: a low-cost housing scheme		26
The Barbican: a high-cost housing scheme		27
3 Employment		29
Offices		30
Retailing		38
Tourism and recreation		41
Manufacturing industry		45
Dockland		47
4 Transport		54
Railways		54
London Regional Transport		56
Waterways		57
Roads		57
Airports		60
5 London's physical environment		63
Water supply		63
Flooding		63
Sewers		66
Air pollution		66
6 Administering and planning London		68
Administering London		68
Planning the London region: the 1944 Greater London Plan		70
South-East Study 1961–1981		71
Strategic Plan for the South–East 1981–2000		71
The Green Belt		73
7 Conclusion: inner/outer, east/west contrasts		75
8 Data sources		77
Libraries		77
Local authorities		77
Census data		77
Other useful sources		78
Books		78
Acknowledgements		79
Index		80

Series preface

Alvin Toffler, in his book *Future Shock*, examined the effects of the increasing pace of change in modern society. The speed of change in modern geographical education is no exception. The methodology of the Quantitative Revolution is now set alongside the more challenging framework of the People–Environment approach and value-based learning. In addition, the nature of the sixth form has changed so that the traditional Advanced level student is not the sole type of student. Sixth form and tertiary colleges teaching large groups, and the increasing numbers of students in the 'New Sixth' studying for BEC and similar awards, are common today.

In addition, regrettably, only a small proportion of geographers at 16–19 actually proceed to take the subject in further education, although it remains one of the most popular sixth form subjects. These contrasting demands have influenced the thinking behind this series of short texts aimed at the modern student, ninety per cent of whom will not pursue geography beyond the sixth form. We have assumed that the readers will have taken all forms of GCSE geography examinations although the content should present no difficulties for the more mature reader. In all the texts it is our intention that the author's enthusiasm for the topic, combined with the interest generated by the presentation of the text, will assist a wide range of learners in and out of the classroom. The subject matter presents the challenges which our society and environment will face in the 1990s in a format that stimulates debate and understanding of the issues and the problems facing our rapidly changing world.

Every text can be studied in isolation, which should suit the individual curriculum of any group. Therefore, there is little attempt to cross reference texts which might be used in different order by schools and colleges. In addition, a self-standing set of texts leaves topic selection within a syllabus to the teacher's discretion. Nevertheless, the texts develop new views of the more traditional sections of geography and introduce others where available material at this level is limited.

All the authors have a common concern for the improvement of geography teaching to the 16–19 group as experienced teachers, lecturers and examiners. All try to build on existing knowledge of our environment and to stress the dynamic nature of the environment. Where possible, they have asked the reader to express attitudes and explain values towards the major issues which affect our social, economic and physical environment. Above all, the authors are aware of geography's continuing role in teaching people how to think.

David Burtenshaw
Waterlooville 1988

London in the 1980s

It was an important decade in the history of London. Serious riots flared in areas settled by large numbers of disadvantaged ethnic groups. Problems of housing, unemployment and police-community relations had rarely seemed worse. The number of Londoners continued to decline while, for the first time since 1855, the city found itself without an overall governing body. Two major airport projects were initiated, one in the very heart of the conurbation. The first ring-road to be built around London was completed. A miniature Hong Kong began to emerge out of the desolation of abandoned dockland, and the decade saw fundamental changes in the financial heart of London.

One in seven of the people of England and Wales live in London. With a population of 6.78 million in 1987, London was bigger than the combined totals of the next fifteen biggest cities in the UK (6.75 m) or the whole of Denmark (5.1 m). By the middle of the decade the value of property in London represented a quarter of the total for England and Wales. If the residential population of London has been declining, its importance as a focus for so much in national life has not. Politically, economically and culturally, the dominance of London remains relatively undiminished.

London

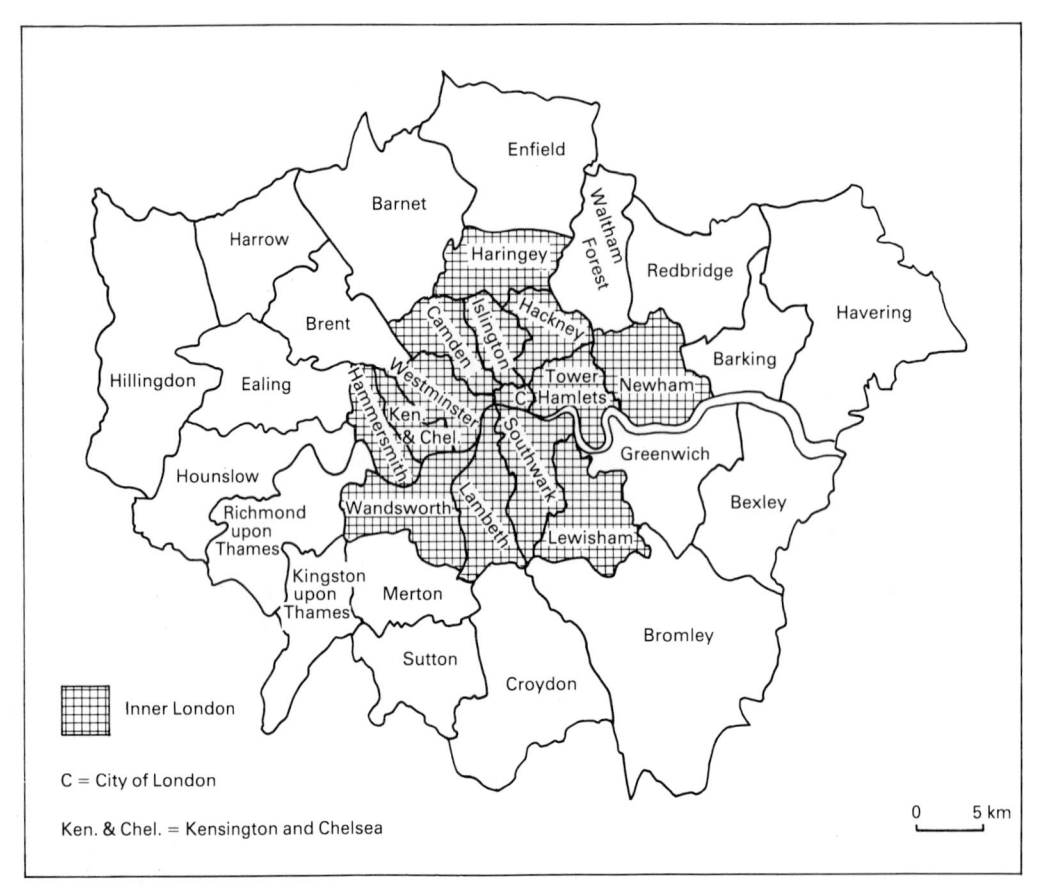

Figure 1.1 London boroughs

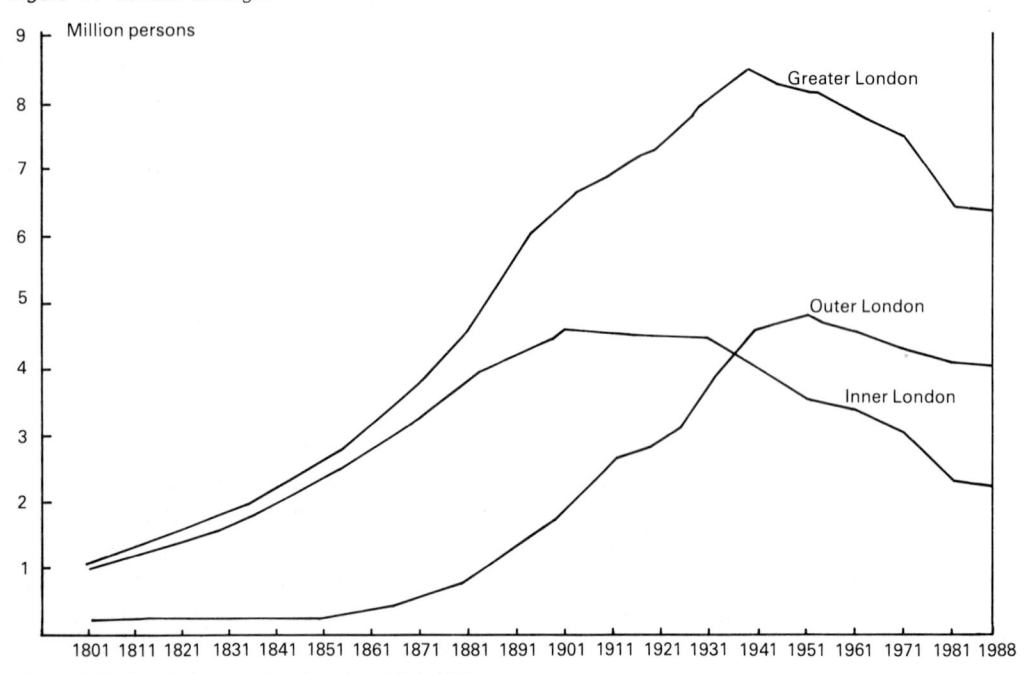

Figure 1.2 Population trends in London, 1801–1988

1
People

With 6.78 million people in 1987, London was the ninth largest city in the world. London and the south–east of England had a combined population of 16.7 million, over 30% of the British people. Easily the most cosmopolitan city in Britain, London is the home of some of the richest as well as some of the most disadvantaged groups. Changing social values and standards of living have been reflected in the lifestyles and composition of the city's population. Like all great cities, London both reflects and generates changes in the wider society of which it is a part.

Population change

The population of London has been declining for several years. The original central square mile of London, now known as the City (Figure 1.1), fell from a peak of 129,000 people in 1807 to less than 5000 by 1981. The population of inner boroughs declined after 1901, while that of Greater London as a whole fell from a peak of 8.6 in 1939 to 6.7 in 1981. Between 1971 and 1981 the total population of Greater London fell by 10.3%, but the inner boroughs fell by 18% (Figure 1.2). This compares with an overall increase of 0.5% for England and Wales.

Those parts of London which were built first have, therefore, been the first to lose population. As if a stone had been cast into the centre of a pond, a ripple of growth has moved outwards, to be followed by a trough of decline.

The population of the central area, the City, has shown a slight increase in recent years with the completion of the Barbican development (page 27). The population of other parts of London continued to fall until 1984, since when both inner and outer London have registered a slight increase.

The population decline seen in London has occurred in a similar way in virtually all cities, and many large towns, throughout Western Europe and North America in recent years – a phenomenon known as **counterurbanisation**. The processes responsible for it can be divided into three groups:

(i) **Positive:** forces which *attract* people and employment to regions surrounding cities. People are drawn by cheaper housing, greater space, a more pleasant living environment and growing job opportunities in these areas. Industrial, retail and office land uses are attracted out of the city centres to the cheaper land and therefore greater space, the proximity of motorways or airports, the availability of new factories on green-field sites, and lower average wage rates. A specific magnet has been the new and expanded towns created by various governments since the war (page 70).

(ii) **Negative:** forces which *push* people and jobs out of cities – inflated property prices, high rates, congestion, poor schools, unemployment, rising crime levels and a poor living environment for families with children. Commerce may be discouraged by high rents, lack of space to expand and labour costs. Demolition of houses and old factory premises, and the comprehensive redevelopment schemes of the 1950s and 1960s, have also displaced large numbers to new estates outside London.

London

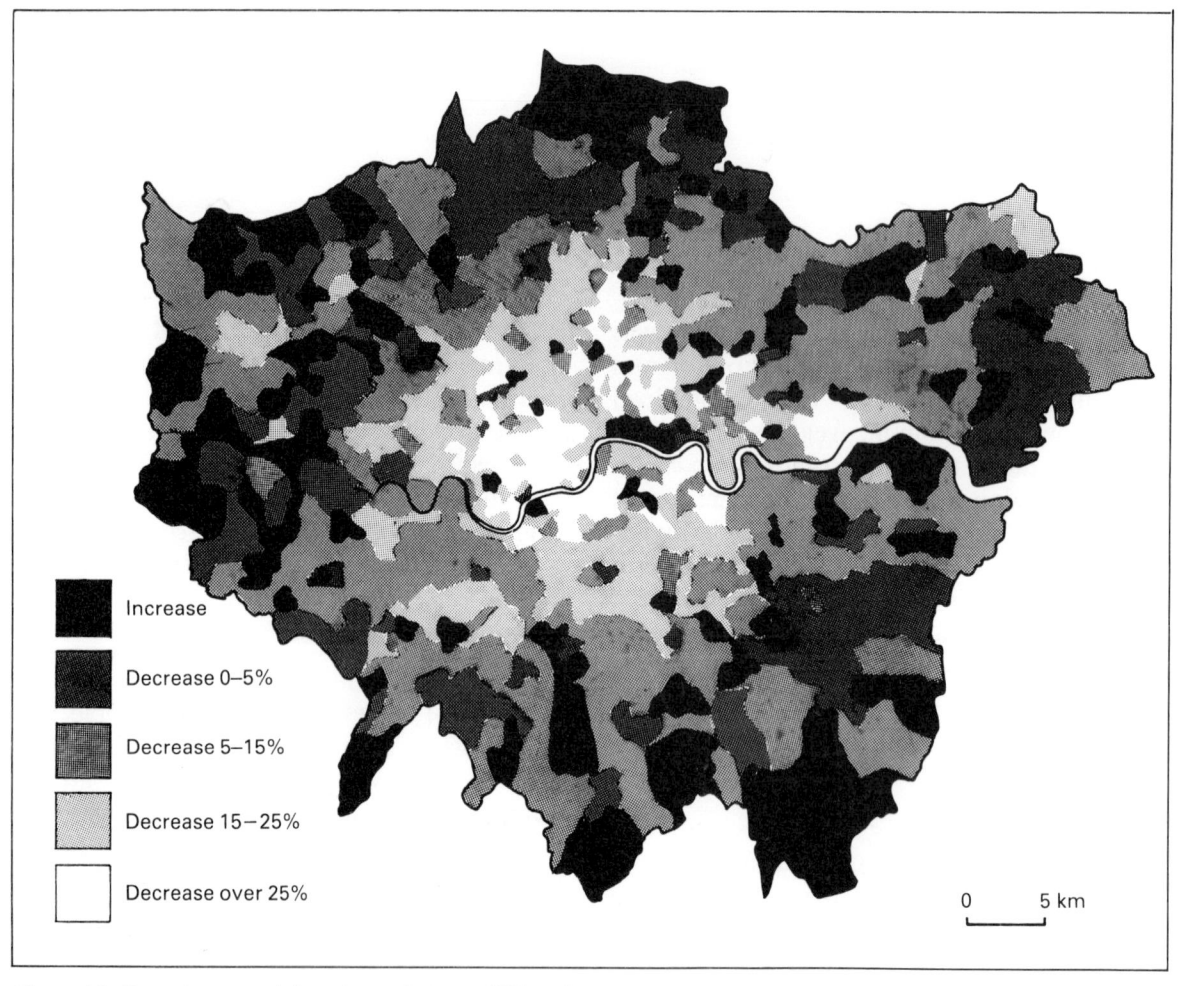

Figure 1.3 *Percentage population change between 1971 and 1981*

Legend:
- Increase
- Decrease 0–5%
- Decrease 5–15%
- Decrease 15–25%
- Decrease over 25%

(iii) **Neutral:** forces which *permit* people or jobs to locate outside the city. Improved transport has enabled many to live outside London but commute to work in it. Similarly, good telecommunications services allow firms to establish offices or factories in outer areas while retaining contact with a head office in London.

One important reason for the falling population is the changing household structure of London. In 1981, 32% of the households of inner London, and 22% of the households of outer London consisted of one person living alone (Figure 1.4). Single people and small families are now occupying houses once lived in by larger families with servants. As standards of living have risen, more young people have been able to rent or buy their own home. To some extent they have been forced to do the latter by a decline in the available amount of privately rented accommodation. The average family size has also fallen, and a rising divorce rate has increased the number of people living alone. The elderly make up an increasing proportion of London's population and in 1981 38% of women of pensionable age in London lived alone.

People

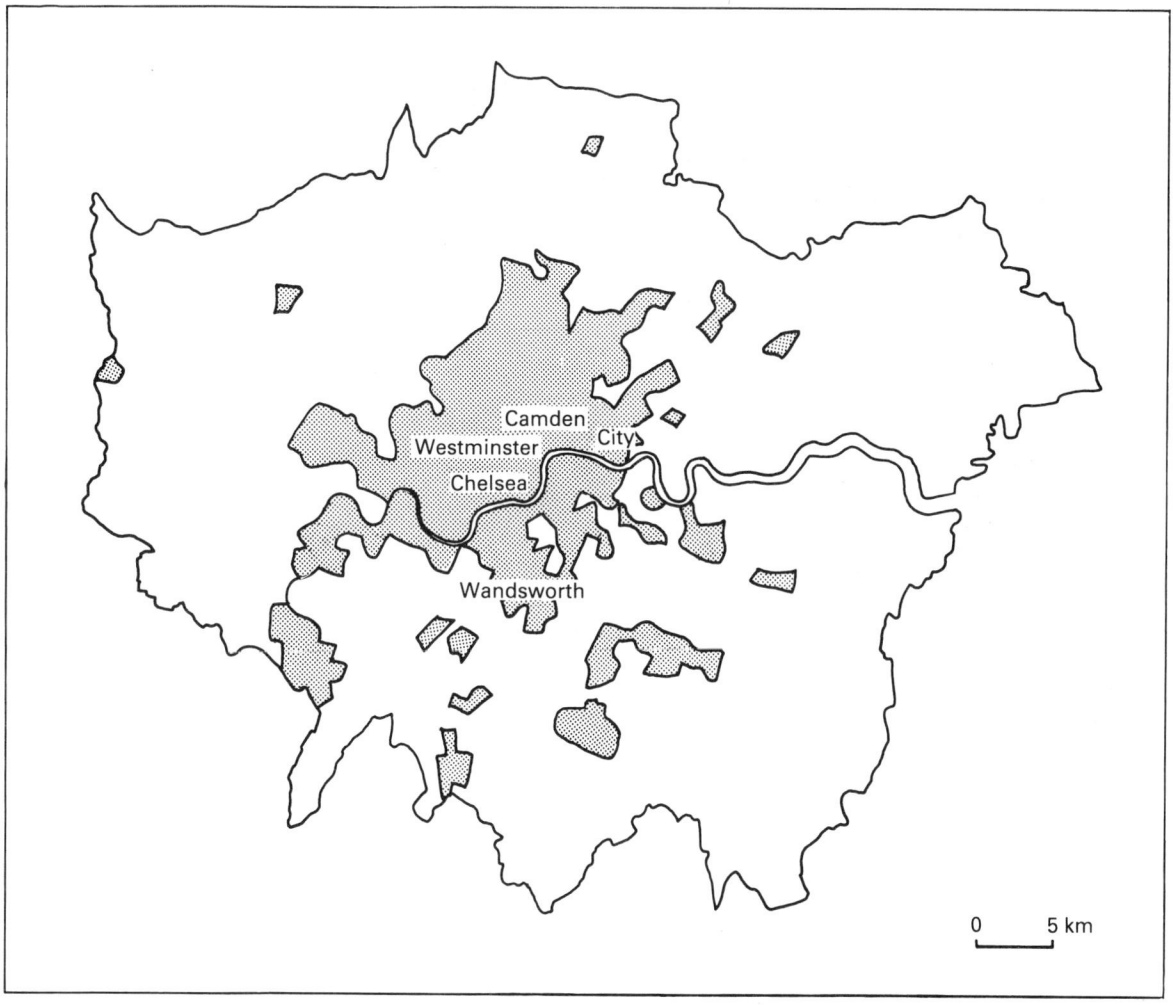

Figure 1.4 Areas where over 30% of households consisted of only one person, 1981

Study questions

1 Which would you prefer to live in, a city like London or a rural village? Summarise the advantages and disadvantages of both.
2 Is the population decline of London a good thing? What could the government do to halt it?
3 Write a paragraph on 'the geography of loneliness' (the distribution of people who live alone).

Age and sex structure

London has proportionately more young adults (20–30 age group) than the rest of the country. The largest numbers are found in a discontinuous ring around inner London. The type of housing available here caters for the needs of those starting their first job: privately rented accommodation, often in the form of small flats. Young adults are often unable or unwilling to pay for commuting, preferring to live near to the social and leisure opportunities offered by central London.

Studies of the life-cycles of individuals show

London

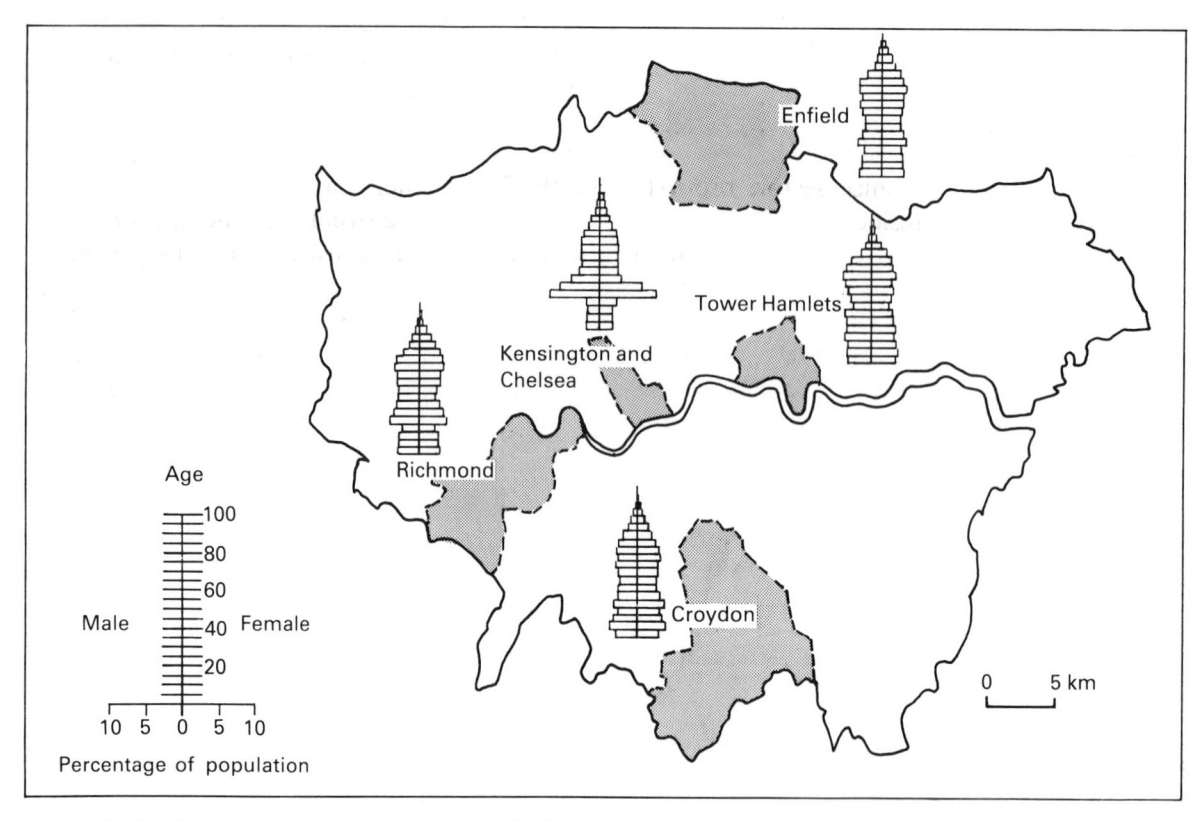

Figure 1.5 Population pyramids showing the age–sex structure of five representative boroughs, 1981

that, while many young people start their working lives in inner London, once married they prefer to move out to the suburbs and beyond where houses are cheaper and the environment more suitable for bringing up children. This movement is reflected in differences between the age structures of people living in inner and outer London (Figure 1.5).

The years 1971–81 saw a fall in the proportion of London's population under 16, a consequence of the falling birth rate. Although London still has proportionately fewer children than the country as a whole, the number of very young children (0–4 years) rose by 21% between 1981 and 1984, much of this increase being due to the high birth rate amongst Asian communities.

During this period there was also a rise in the proportion of London's pensioners (women over 60, men over 65); the highest proportion is to be found in some of the older, inner suburbs, such as Richmond (Figure 1.5).

In all parts of London there are more females than males. The sex ratio becomes more imbalanced the closer one goes to the centre. In Kensington and Chelsea, for example, 54.2% of the population were female in 1981 (Figure 1.5). Much of this imbalance is created by the selective migration of young working women to inner areas, where there are more job opportunities for women, as well as a good supply of privately rented accommodation.

Study question

Can you think of any other places in, or outside, Britain where sex ratios are imbalanced? Why does such an imbalance exist?

People

Population density

Residential densities (see Figure 1.6) are lowest in the centre of London – the City – at 21 persons per hectare in 1981. Because of demand for this land from the office sector, property prices are too high for residential use.

Densities rise rapidly outside the City, to 78 persons per hectare in inner London, falling in the suburbs to 33 persons per hectare. Houses in inner London are older, and those built before 1914 tend to be closer together (for example, the large proportion of terraced housing). Land values in inner areas are higher, so people are obliged to live in less space. Furthermore, there is a higher proportion of low earners in the inner areas: 43% of households in inner London were in council accommodation in 1981, compared with 23% in outer London.

Because of the overall decline in population described above, densities are falling throughout London, most rapidly in the inner areas. The most dramatic change in the period 1971 to 1981 occurred in the borough of Kensington and Chelsea, where population density fell from 158 to 116 persons per hectare.

Figure 1.6 Population density, 1981

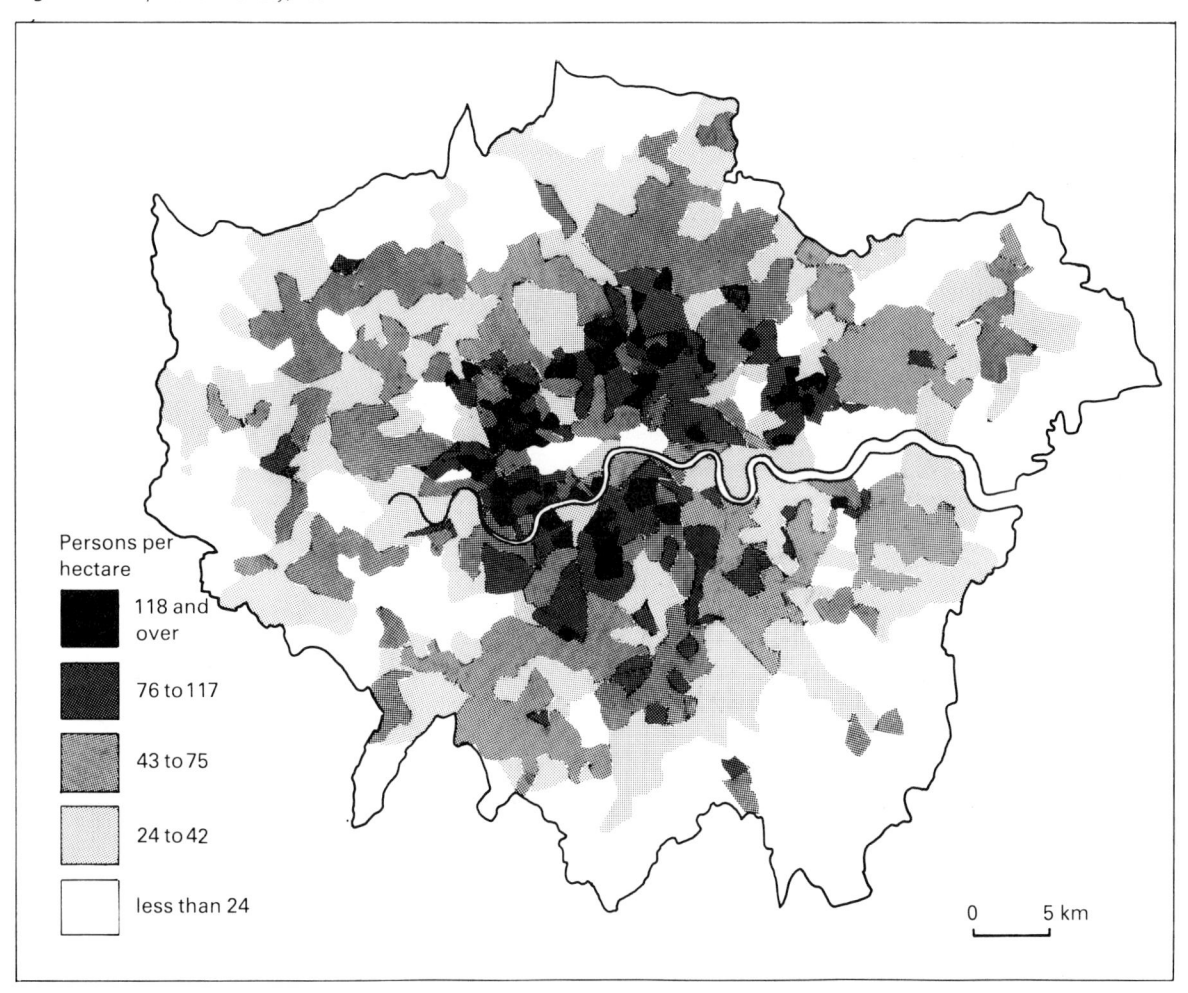

London

Socio-economic groups

It is the distribution of people with differing incomes and jobs which most clearly characterises different parts of London and gives Londoners their mental images of the capital.

The greatest concentration of the **lower paid** is found in the East End (Figure 1.7). This is the area where, between 1802 and 1921, the great dock basins were constructed. A huge workforce was needed to build and run the docks, as well as to man the many industries which developed around them, and poorer people could not afford to travel far to work. This was especially true in the eighteenth and nineteenth centuries, when many men were casual labourers, queuing each day outside docks, factories and markets for short-term jobs.

In the east of London, land was divided up into smaller estates than in the west. These were more easily purchased by less wealthy developers and tended, as a result, to have housing of a lower quality built on them. The pattern of income groups therefore perpetuated itself through the housing system. In the East End of London thousands of small terraced cottages were built at high densities to house Victorian workers. Today many of these have been demolished, only to be replaced by council flats.

The western side of London developed around Westminster. It was here, on Thorney Island, a triangle created by two branches of the river Tyburn as it flowed into the Thames, that the first abbey was built by the Saxon king Sebert in the sixth century AD. Edward the Confessor rebuilt the abbey in the eleventh century, as well as a royal palace; it was this act of placing the royal court on the western side of London which established the west as the fashionable part of the city.

In the seventeenth and eighteenth centuries, the area between St Paul's and the Strand saw the construction of grand houses for courtiers. Much of the land was owned by wealthy landlords, such as the Duke of Bedford, the Grosvenor family or the Crown. They were anxious to maintain the status of the area by building houses for the relatively prosperous. Once the West End had gained this reputation it maintained it, extending westwards along the Thames as the most fashionable part of London.

Much of outer west and south-east London has since attracted the **professional and managerial** classes. Here the pleasant environment, cost of commuting and value of housing have combined to produce areas of above-average status (Figure 1.8).

Figure 1.7 Areas where over 10% of the employed population were unskilled manual workers, 1981

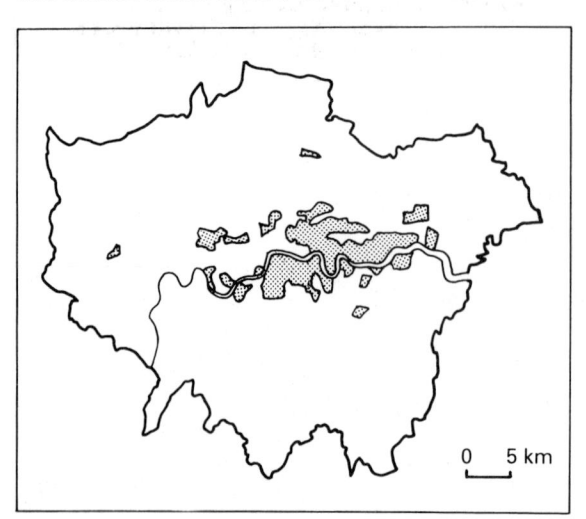

Figure 1.8 Areas where over 20% of the employed population were professional or managerial workers, 1981

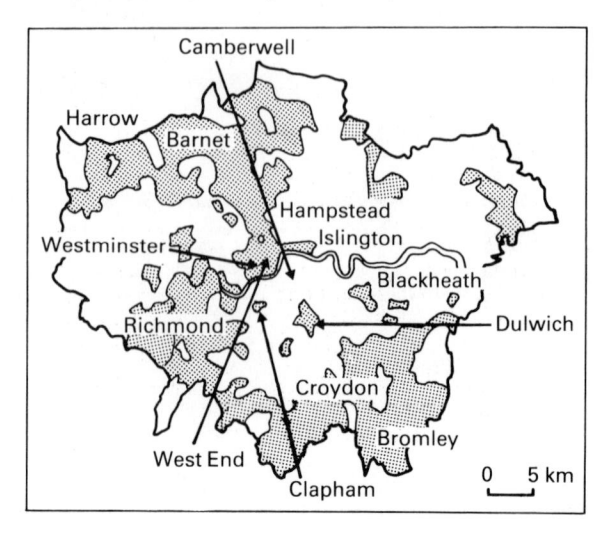

Many of the most expensive parts of London are established as the home of the prosperous. Three types of area are particularly important:

(i) Streets around parks or commons, such as Greenwich, Blackheath or Richmond in south London.

(ii) Hills, such as Hampstead or Highgate in north London. These originated as rural villages outside London with the advantages of clean air, good views and well-drained land. Hampstead Village became a fashionable spa when chalybeate (iron-rich) springs were discovered there in the eighteenth century.

(iii) Villages which have retained some character as the suburbs have engulfed them. Dulwich, in the south-eastern suburbs, was a seventeenth-century manorial village. In 1613 Edward Alleyn founded Dulwich College, and this school, with its grounds and smart houses in surrounding streets, gives the area particular status.

> **Study activity**
>
> Obtain a description of the Burgess and Hoyt models of urban structure (in any standard text). To what extent does the pattern of people in London correspond to either of these models?

> **Study question**
>
> The following is a description of two villages outside London in 1730. Today, these are fashionable suburbs.
> What made them particularly desirable in the eighteenth century? Why do you think they have kept their status?
>
> HAMPSTEAD.
> This village is situated about four miles on the north-west side of London. It was once very small, but by the increase of buildings is now of considerable extent. Many of the citizens of London have fine houses here, because the situation is not only delightful, but the air is esteemed exceeding wholesome. Here is a public place called the Long Room, where the gentry meet to amuse themselves once a week; and here is also an assembly room 60 feet long and 30 broad, adorned in a very elegant manner. Most of those who reside in the village pay an annual subscription, but others pay 2s. 6d. each time for admittance. On Sundays such as please may meet here and drink tea, but no diversions of any kind are permitted.
> In this village is a very handsome church for the use of the inhabitants; besides which there is a neat chapel, and a meeting-house for protestant dissenters.
> At the north extremity of the village is a heath or common, which is adorned with many handsome buildings, and is so elevated, as to command one of the most extensive prospects in the kingdom. At the bottom of the heath, towards Highgate, is Caen-wood, where there is a handsome seat belonging to the right hon. earl Mansfield.
>
> HIGHGATE.
> This is a large straggling village, between four and five miles north of London, and is so called from its situation on a hill, and from a gate which was erected by the bishop of London upwards of 400 years ago, where a toll was paid by carriages, as the road at that time ran through a part of the bishop's park. This gate, however, has been taken down some years, and the road laid entirely open.
> The church, which is a very old structure, is only a chapel of ease to Hornsey. On the spot where it stands was antiently a small hermitage, near which the lord chief baron Cholmondeley built and endowed a free-school in 1562, which was enlarged in 1570 by Edwin Sandys, bishop of London, and a chapel added to it but all remains of these have been long extinct.
> Highgate is a very populous village, and in it are many handsome seats belonging to the gentry and others. The prospect from hence over London and the river Thames, together with the counties of Surry, and Kent, is really astonishing; and the variety of objects which present themselves to the sight, fills the mind of the spectator with admiration.
>
> From William Thornton's *History of London*

London

Not all parts of London have remained the preserve of just one social group since the day they were built. In the Victorian era more middle-class houses were constructed by hopeful developers than could be matched by demand. Brixton, for example, was built for the carriage-owning class, but lost status once the railway enabled poorer people to live there and commute to the centre.

A well-known example of an area which lost its status and then regained it is Barnsbury, in Islington. Built between 1820 and 1850 for the middle classes, this area lost status after 1880 as the original residents moved further out of London in search of more modern and spacious homes. Properties were sub-divided, and working-class residents moved in. Since 1960, a shortage of good housing near central London has encouraged a reversal of this trend, with the middle classes moving back into an area which had retained some architectural quality. The 1969 Housing Act made **home improvement grants** available to people who could afford to finance some of the improvement work on their houses themselves. This produced **gentrification** or **filtering-up**, and the area returned to relative prosperity – with a concomitant rise in the value of properties. In the 1970s and 1980s this process happened in many areas of inner London, notably Camberwell and Clapham, both typical middle-class Victorian suburbs.

> **Study activity**
>
> Find an area of housing which you know has undergone gentrification in recent years. Ask local people how the area has changed in terms of:
> - the average age and income of people living there
> - the appearance of the houses
> - the price of properties
> - the types of shops
>
> In what respects can gentrification be regarded as *un*desirable?

Figure 1.9 Gentrification in progress, Spitalfields

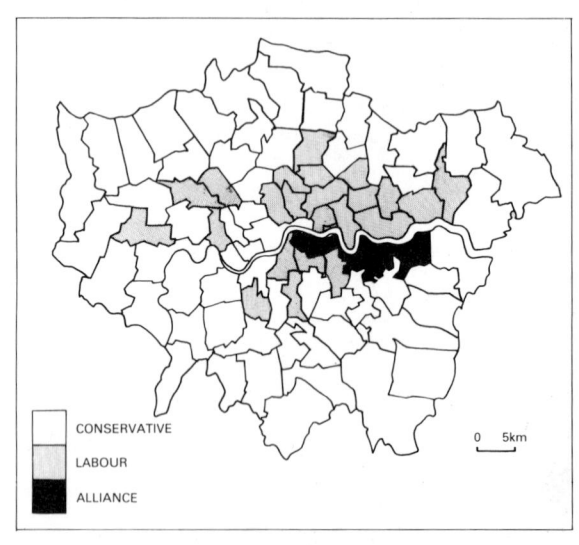

Figure 1.10 Results of the general election, June 1987

> **Study question**
>
> Describe the pattern of voting in the 1987 general election (Figure 1.10). Explain this pattern, referring to Figures 1.7 and 1.8.

People

Ethnic groups

A high proportion of immigrants who have come to settle in Britain live in London. London is the place that an immigrant is likely to know most about. More jobs and opportunities have normally been available in London than in other cities, and it has often been the port of arrival for immigrants coming to Britain.

The **Irish** came over in large numbers after the potato famine of 1845. They live in particularly large numbers in inner boroughs of north and west London (Figure 1.11). However, most parts of London have some Irish living in them, and it is this spread which distinguishes them from other minority ethnic groups. It is a reflection of their greater degree of **assimilation** – they have become better absorbed into British society over a long period of time.

Jews came to Britain in the period 1880–1914, fleeing religious persecution in Eastern Europe, and again in the 1930s when they were driven out of Germany by the Nazis. Of 300,000 members of the Anglo-Jewish community in Britain in 1980, two-thirds lived in London. In the nineteenth century most Jews settled in inner London, especially the East End. In the present century the Jewish community has tended to move to the outer suburbs of north London, especially Barnet and Golders Green (Figure 1.12). This was a reflection of their rising economic status.

The orthodox Jewish community has remained more segregated than some other minority groups. Many Jews have retained their religion, traditions and strong sense of family loyalty. They need to cluster in order to support, and have access to, Jewish institutions: synagogues, Jewish day schools, shops selling food which corresponds to Jewish dietary laws, and Jewish cemeteries. Religious law forbids orthodox Jews to travel by any means other than on foot on the sabbath and other holy days, so they need to live near these institutions. A high proportion of Jews marry other Jews (**endogamy** – marriage within the group), and this also helps to maintain segregation.

Many immigrants to London have come from India, Bangladesh, Pakistan, Commonwealth African countries and the Caribbean. In 1981, about 890,000 Londoners had such an ethnic origin. Over a third of these were born in the UK, and many of the rest had arrived in the period 1948–68. They came to England because of unemployment, overpopulation and rural poverty in their home countries, combined with a demand for labour in Britain. Many were actively encouraged to come to England by

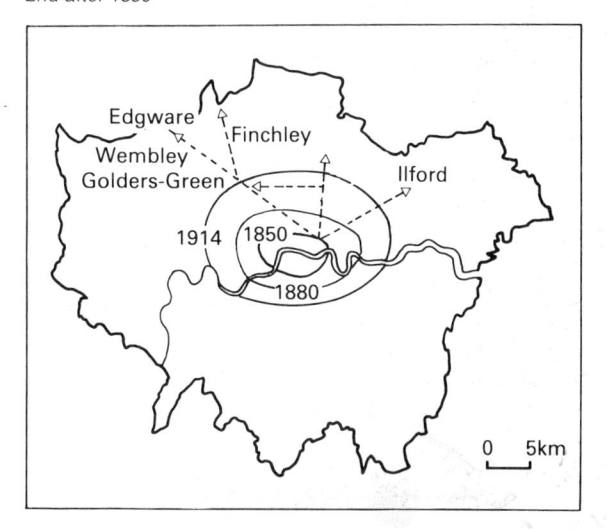

Figure 1.11 Areas where over 9% of residents were born in the Irish Republic, 1981

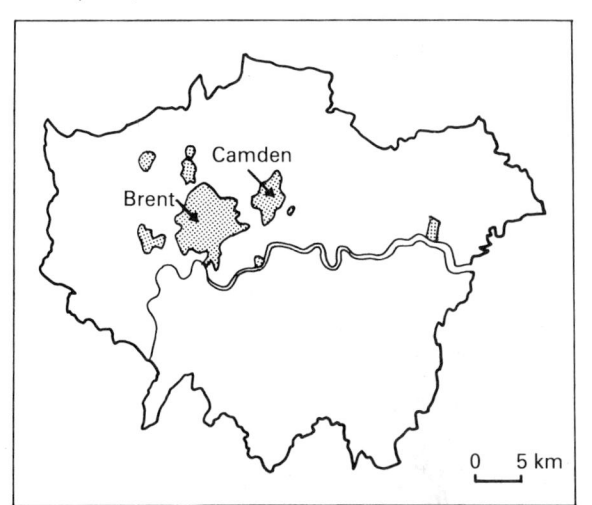

Figure 1.12 Movement of the Jewish community out of the East End after 1850

London

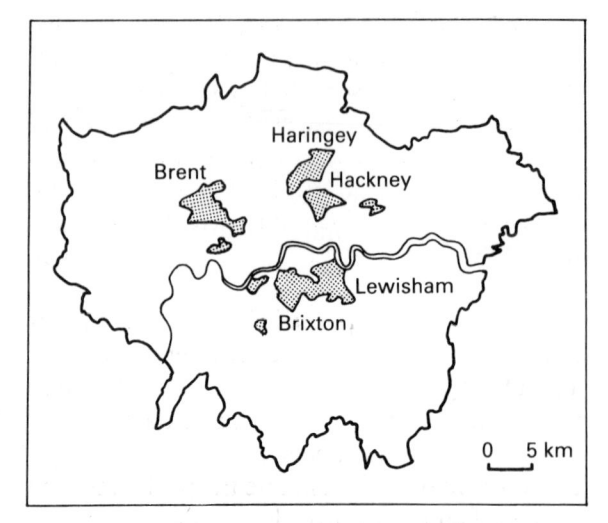

Figure 1.13 Areas where over 6% of the residents were born in the Caribbean, 1981

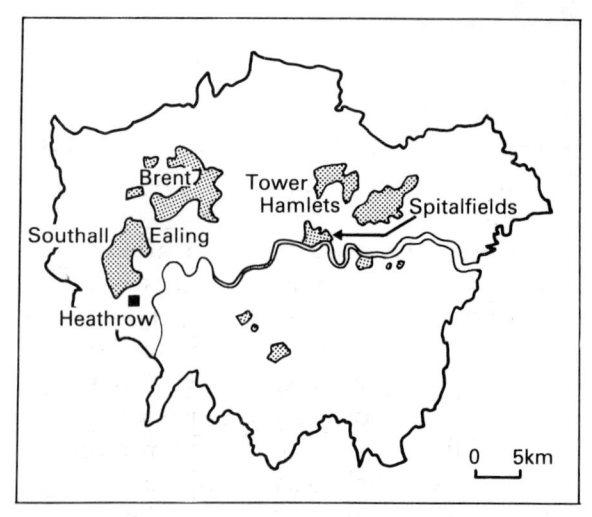

Figure 1.14 Areas where over 6.5% of the residents were born in India, Pakistan or Bangladesh, 1981

employers, such as London Transport, who were short of labour. Most held British passports. Some came because of discrimination or unrest in their home countries. Asians came from Kenya in 1967–8 and Uganda in 1972 because of discrimination against them at home. Refugees of the Vietnam War came in the late 1970s and early 1980s, some seeking political asylum. Acts of Parliament to restrict immigration were passed in 1962, 1968 and 1971. As a result, after 1971 many of the immigrants coming to Britain were dependants of those already settled here.

Within London, immigrants from these countries have concentrated in certain areas. **West Indians** are found mainly in the inner city, with particularly large numbers in Brent, Lambeth, Southwark, Lewisham, Hackney and Haringey. Relatively few live in the outer suburbs. A high proportion of West Indians live in council houses or privately rented accommodation.

Asians are grouped in both inner and outer London. A large number settled in Tower Hamlets, just east of the City. This is a traditional textile quarter and, with their particular skills in this trade, Asians are following in the footsteps of French Huguenots and Jews (Figure 1.15).

Further from the centre, concentrations of Asians are found in the north-eastern and western suburbs. The job opportunities related to Heathrow airport encouraged many to live in Hounslow. Because kinship ties between Asians are so strong, they have been able to pool their savings in order to buy houses. A higher proportion of Asians than West Indians are home owners.

Asian and Afro-Caribbean immigrants in Britain do not generally form high-density

Figure 1.15 This building, on the corner of Brick Lane in Spitalfields, was once a French Huguenot chapel, later a Jewish synagogue. Today it is an Asian mosque

ghettos of the type found in American cities, although a few small-scale concentrations do exist. The highest immigrant proportion is presently found in Brent, where over half the population is non-white. The groupings which exist do so for a number of reasons. The type of housing immigrants live in is itself clustered. The cheap, privately rented accommodation sought by early West Indian immigrants, for example, is concentrated in less prosperous parts of inner London. Many immigrants need to live near their jobs, especially when, as with those manning public transport, they work unsocial hours.

In addition, it was natural for members of these groups to stick together, especially Asians who spoke only limited English. Many immigrants arriving in London chose to live with or near people they knew from their home country. For this reason some small parts of London contain large numbers from individual Asian villages. In Southall, for example, a high proportion of immigrants came from the Jullundur and Hoshiarpur regions of the Punjab, which had been important recruiting areas for the British-run Indian army after 1857 (Figure 1.16). Links between the area and Britain were, therefore, strong. The attraction of Southall was the availability of jobs, particularly in Woolf's Rubber Company: in 1965, 90% of its unskilled workers were Sikhs. Grouping together enabled these communities to support ethnic institutions such as Asian shops, mosques and temples.

To some extent, segregation has also been an inevitable response to racial discrimination. A Home Office report in 1981 concluded that Asians were fifty times more likely to be attacked than whites, and that the number of such attacks was growing.

Riots in Brixton in April 1981 seemed to focus attention on the problems of immigrants in Britain. During the disturbances, 279 people were injured and £6.4 million worth of damage was caused. The government appointed a judge, Lord Scarman, to investigate the problems, and he identified three particular issues:

(i) Insensitive police behaviour. Prior to the riots, the police had been deployed in unusually large numbers as part of an operation to combat street crime in the area.

(ii) Higher than average levels of unemployment amongst blacks, particularly young blacks. In April 1981, 55% of black males under 19 were employed.

(iii) Poor housing in the affected areas. In 1977, 20% of houses in Lambeth were substandard (overcrowded or unfit).

Figure 1.16 Areas of origin of many Asian immigrants to Southall

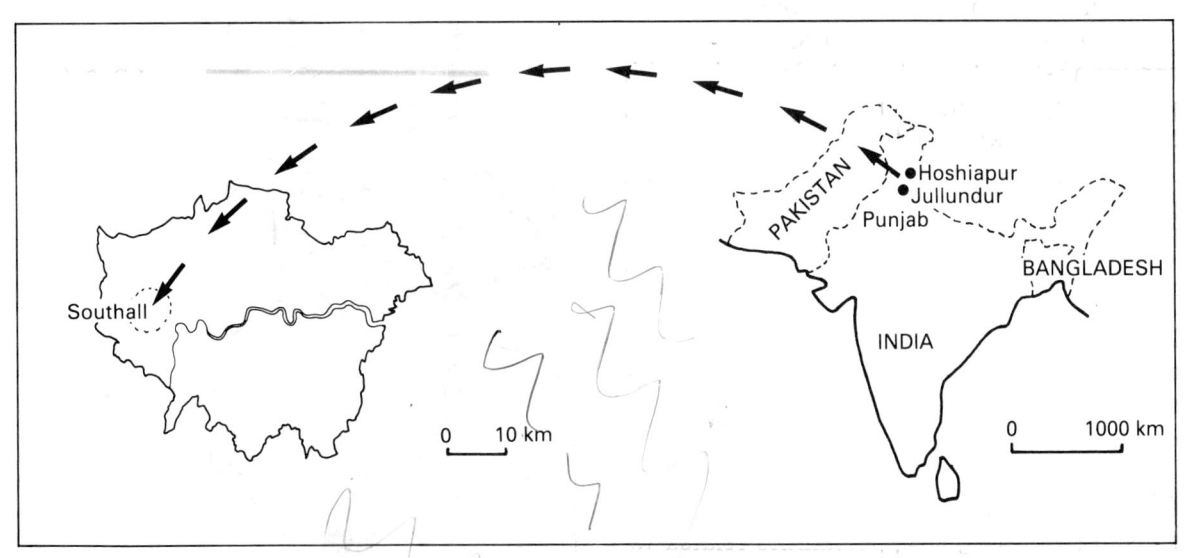

London

In addition, Scarman was concerned about the instability of family life amongst West Indians (twice the national average of single-parent families), and about institutional racism: '...practices may be adopted by public bodies as well as by private individuals which are unwittingly discriminating against black people....'

Scarman recommended a number of reforms. Police procedure and training should be improved, and the police force should recruit more blacks. Housing, education and employment opportunities in the area needed to be greatly improved, and the people should also receive more attention from Community Relations Councils.

The autumn of 1985 saw further rioting in Peckham, Tottenham and Brixton. In Brixton 99 cars were burnt, 83 shops looted, two women were raped and 220 people arrested. On the Broadwater Farm estate in Tottenham, where half the population was black and unemployment exceeded 40%, a man was killed.

Study question

What do you think should be done, in concrete terms, to solve the problems of discontent amongst immigrant groups in areas such as Brixton? Ask yourself what factors might be influencing your opinions (your family, friends, politics, etc.).

Figure 1.17 Brixton riots in April 1981

Inner city aid

The 1981 Census showed that of all local authorities in England, Tower Hamlets had the worst overcrowding, the definition of which (more than 1.5 people per room) covered 10% of households, Hammersmith had the most households lacking basic amenities (15.2% without exclusive use of a bath and inside WC), and Kensington had the highest population loss (26.2% between 1971 and 1981). Parts of inner London are therefore amongst the most disadvantaged in Britain. Socially, they suffer from high levels of homelessness, crime, mental illness (Figure 1.18), above-average numbers of single-parent families, and low levels of educational achievement. Economically, they have experienced the fastest decline in job opportunities and are characterised by high unemployment. Environmentally, they have a large proportion of unfit housing and derelict land. They also have the greatest numbers of low income groups and immigrants. Taken together, these problems create conditions of **multiple deprivation**.

Within London, an early attempt to deal with the educational aspects of multiple deprivation came with the **Plowden Report on Children and their Primary Schools**, in 1966. The report advised the government to give extra assistance to schools in poorer areas, and in 1968 the Inner London Education Authority (ILEA) established **Educational Priority Areas** to do this. Even so, in the mid-1980s 21% of children from inner London left school with no formal qualifications, compared with 11% in outer London and 7.5% in the Home Counties.

More significant has been the **urban programme** of aid, initiated by the 1978 **Inner Urban Areas Act**, and a response to the Inner Area Studies undertaken by the Department of the Environment in 1976 in London, Liverpool and Birmingham. The Act provides for additional finance to local authorities in inner-city areas. The money is given to both private firms and public sector investment schemes in order to create jobs, improve housing and rejuvenate the environment.

People

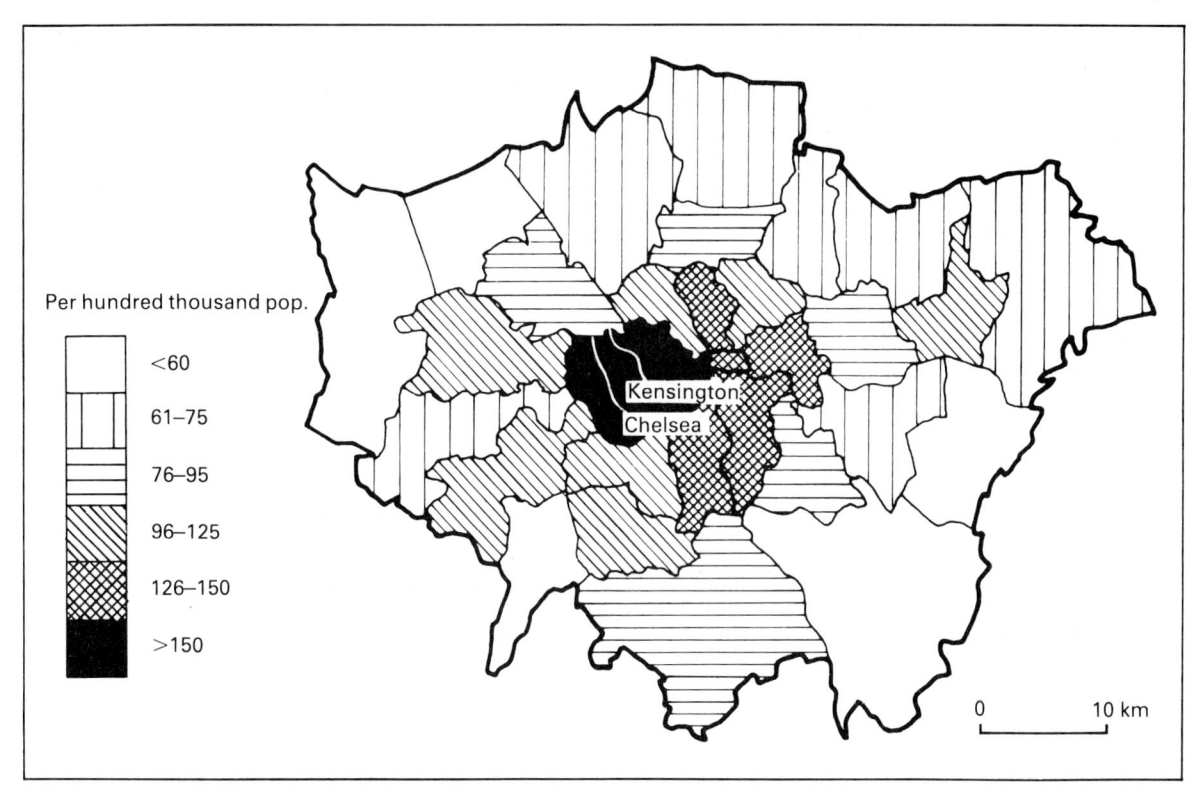

Figure 1.18 Distribution of patients admitted to psychiatric hospitals suffering from schizophrenia in London 1976

A three-tier system of assistance was set up: **Partnership Authorities**, in which the local authority works in partnership with central government and receives grants of up to 75% of the cost of approved schemes, **Programme Authorities**, who also receive grants for specific projects, and **Designated Districts**, which obtain grants for industrial and economic projects only (Table 1.1). The 11-hectare site of the former Wandsworth gasworks, for example, is inside a Programme Authority. Here, the old gasworks machinery has been cleared and small industrial units are being built to act as premises for local people wanting to start their own businesses. The units are being built by the private sector, but the companies behind the project receive a grant (called an **Urban Development Grant**) from the Department of the Environment. Much money has been spent on environmental projects, many quite small, such as the William Curtis Ecological Park on a patch of derelict land near Tower Bridge.

In 1986 the government appointed special **task forces** to help two areas of London which had particularly large numbers of unemployed young people: Notting Hill and North Peckham. The task forces will work with local authorities, communities and voluntary agencies to encourage private enterprise jobs and training schemes for young people.

Table 1.1 Areas receiving assistance, under the 1978 Inner Urban Areas Act, in 1986

Partnership Authorities	Programme Authorities	Designated Districts
Hackney	Brent	Ealing
Lambeth	Hammersmith	Greenwich
Islington	Tower Hamlets	Haringey
	Wandsworth	Lewisham
		Newham
		Southwark

London

> **Study question**
>
> Inner urban areas have higher levels of crime, family breakdown and mental illness (Figure 1.18) than outer areas. What possible reasons could there be for this? Consider two possibilities: a) inner areas attract larger numbers of criminals, single-parent families etc. to live there, and b) the social and physical environment of inner areas *causes* such problems. Add any other reasons you can think of.

Crime

Between 1960 and 1985 the number of recorded crimes in London rose by 400–500%. It is hard to tell to what extent this was due to improved recording by the Metropolitan Police, but there is little doubt that it represented a worsening problem.

Detailed research on the issue was undertaken by the Islington Crime Survey in 1985. In this area one in two households is a victim of crime each year. One in 11 households is burgled each year, and in 1985 7000 cars were stolen or broken into. The highest rates of burglary occurred in households occupied by ethnic groups, squatters, or those earning over £8000 per annum. One in 40 people was sexually assaulted, including one in 11 young white women. One in 4 women questioned said that she would never go out alone at any time of day.

"Pepys was an estate designed for crime", says Hugh Smith, of the Safe Neighbourhood Unit, the group called in by the Greater London Council to try to solve the problems. Corridors were used as footways, and front doors, many largely glazed, opened on to them. "It was possible to be inside a flat in a matter of minutes". Smith says. "If people heard a noise, they would be frightened to look out."

Nowhere on the estate was safe. Mrs Wiggins, aged 66, told how she had her pension snatched outside her front door. A woman at the end of the same corridor was burgled three times.

Those who committed crime could quickly make their escape. In the fashion of the day, Pepys was built with 10 interconnected eight-storey blocks and three 24-storey tower blocks. It was a rabbit warren of passages. By the early 1980s many of the original 4,500 inhabitants had left, their places taken by the statutorily rehoused and squatters. Finally the caretakers moved out to central offices in the Old Kent Road.

> **Study question**
>
> The following newspaper extract describes the problem of crime in a modern housing estate in south London. Can you suggest ways in which levels of crime on this estate could be reduced (e.g. policing methods, action by the residents, changes in the design of the buildings – see page 22).

> **Revision**
>
> 1 Why has the population of London declined in recent years?
> 2 What are the main characteristics of the distribution of high and low income groups in London?
> 3 What main factors account for the location of the different immigrant groups in London?
> 4 What is being done about the problem of unemployment in inner London? Do you think the measures will work?

2
Housing

Housing problems

Despite a falling population there is a shortage of good housing in London. Different types of housing have different problems. Many properties are simply old and poorly maintained. Thirty-seven per cent of the capital's houses date from before the First World War, compared with 29% in England and Wales as a whole. In 1984, 210,000 homes were regarded as 'unfit for human habitation' and 354,000 were in a state of serious disrepair. In addition, 128,000 were fit but lacked basic amenities such as an inside lavatory or bath (Figure 2.1). Poor housing is not confined to inner-city areas, but it is disproportionately concentrated in them.

Problems have been caused by **deck-access housing**, some dating from between the wars, but much built in the past 25 years (Figure 2.2). This type of housing is notoriously unpopular. Residents lack any private area outside their front door. The decks have proved to be insecure places, difficult to police and with high incidences of muggings and burglary.

A third type of housing problem has been tall blocks of flats (**point blocks**). Many were built in the period 1955–70 as part of **comprehensive redevelopment** schemes, in which areas of working-class Victorian housing were demolished to make way for the new flats. Planners in the 1960s were influenced by the ideas of the French architect Le Corbusier and the Modern Architecture Research group (MARS), who saw tall buildings as an efficient way of housing people at high densities. Because of the housing shortage, governments of the day encouraged

Figure 2.1 Areas where more than 10% of households lacked exclusive use of both a bath and inside WC, 1981

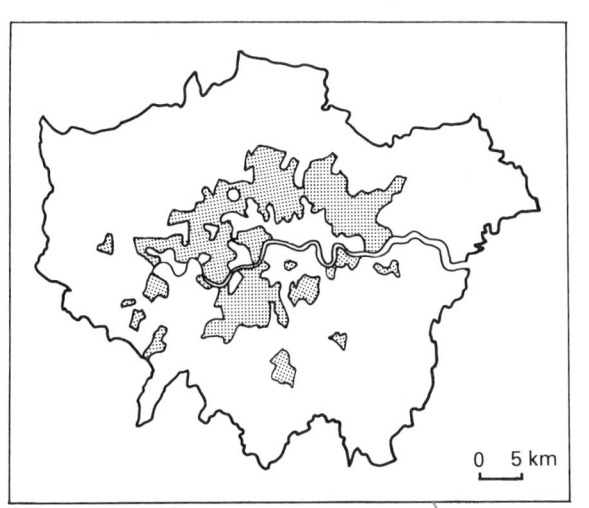

Figure 2.2 Deck-access housing in Rotherhithe

this architectural style: large numbers of flats could be built quickly, and this enabled ministers to fulfil promises made to the electorate. A tall buildings subsidy was introduced to make flats even more attractive to developers. A high proportion of the new flats was built by local authorities as public sector rented housing. This was especially the case in inner London: of the 1080 blocks of flats over nine storeys high in London in 1985, 720 were in inner areas.

By the end of the 1960s this architectural style had already fallen from favour. Comprehensive redevelopment had destroyed many close-knit working-class communities: people living in the new flats lost any feeling of community identity. Residents missed the small gardens or backyards of their old homes as well as the social contact which living in a street afforded. The flats were poorly maintained: lifts broke and the public areas were easily vandalised. Such properties were especially unsuitable for old people and children in ways which seem obvious in retrospect.

Most post-war flats were **system-built**, precast sections being assembled on site. As the years passed it became clear that a proportion was structurally unsound: in 1968 a gas explosion at Ronan Point in Canning Town caused the collapse of one whole section of a block. Many flats were damp: residents could not afford to operate expensive underfloor heating, and condensation was a common problem. The areas of grass around the flats were windy, unfriendly and underused.

Alice Coleman and the Design Disadvantagement Team at the Land Use Research Unit, King's College, London have recently completed an analysis of the problems associated with large blocks of flats. In a study of 4000 blocks, mostly in London, the team noted the incidence of litter, graffiti, vandalism and excrement – all pointers to deteriorating conditions. They interviewed residents, and they recorded the number of children from the flats who were in local authority care. The study found that the recorded problems correlated strongly with certain characteristics of blocks of flats, notably:

(i) Where flats created **anonymity**, with residents knowing few other residents even by sight. This happened where blocks were too big, with very large numbers using one entrance. Naturally, this made it impossible for residents to identify strangers, including criminals, in the area.

(ii) Where the design of flats prevented **surveillance**: there were entrances, corridors or areas of open space which could not be watched from the flats or the street.

(ii) Where blocks had many **alternative escape routes** for vandals, such as interconnecting lifts and stairs.

The team found that the problems of vandalism and decay correlated more strongly with the design variables than, say, with poverty or unemployment. Their basic conclusion was simple: 'The best blocks of flats are those that are most like houses.'

The problems with such housing are partly architectural, but they are also social. Some flats were built well enough, but local authorities failed to maintain the common areas adequately, and people who had little pride in their homes did little to improve them. Once a particular housing estate became unpopular, the flats became **hard to let** and were taken by those people who were most desperate. In this way, some estates came to house a disproportionately large number of 'problem families', and a cycle of decline set in. The process is called **labelling**: an area acquires, and then lives up to, a particular image.

In the 1970s, slum clearance schemes and tall blocks were abandoned in favour of the **rehabilitation** of properties: the improvement of existing buildings, as opposed to their demolition (Table 2.1). Areas of poor housing were designed as **Housing Action Areas** and **General Improvement Areas**, receiving mandatory grants for basic repairs and the installation of indoor lavatories and bathrooms. Home improvement grants were made available to individual home owners whose properties needed damp-proofing, major repair or an inside lavatory.

Housing

Table 2.1 Progression of housing in London

```
1800 ─┐
      │  Pimlico built, 1830
      │
      │  Formation of trusts to provide cheap housing
      │  for the poor, e.g. 1862 Peabody Trust
      │
      │  Early railway suburbs, 1850–70
      │
      │  Shaftesbury Avenue and Charing Cross Road
      │  built, 1880s
      │  Early LCC estates in inner London, 1890s
1900 ─┤  Hampstead Garden Suburb built by social
      │  reformer Dame Henrietta Barnett
      │
      │  Large council estates on edge of London
      │    1900–10, e.g. Norbury, south London
      │    1920–38, e.g. Roehampton
      │
      │  Inter-war private housing building boom
      │  Housing and Town Planning Act 1919
      │  (government subsidies to local authority house
      │  building)
      │
      │  Green Belt Act 1938
      │  Second World War (bomb damage) 1939–45
      │  New Towns Act 1946
1950 ─┤      ▲
      │      │
      │                Beginning of property boom
1960 ─┤  Comprehensive
      │  redevelopment  GLC stopped commissioning
      │                new tower blocks, 1964
      │
      │                Civil Amenities Act, 1967
      │                (conservation areas)
      │
      │                Thamesmead plan, 1966
      │
      │                Collapse of Ronan Point
      │      │         block, 1968
      │      ▼
      │      ▲         Housing Act 1969
1970 ─┤                (improvement grants, General
      │                Improvement Areas)
      │
      │
      │                Housing Act 1974 (Housing
      │                Action Areas)
      │  Rehabilitation
      │                Rent Act 1974 (controlling
      │                rents in privately owned
1980 ─┤                houses)
      │
      │
      │                Housing Act 1980 (sale of
      │                council houses)
      │
      │                Barbican, scheme completed,
      │      ▼         1982 (plan dated from 1956)
```

Figure 2.3 The Lea View estate in Hackney, east London, where a run-down estate has been dramatically transformed by a team of community architects (architects who work closely with the local residents). In 1939 Lea View was known as 'Heaven in Hackney', but by 1980 90% of residents wanted to move. Careful rehabilitation has made the estate popular once more.

Deck-access housing is gradually being improved. On one estate in Hackney the top decks have been removed, and pitched roofs put in to replace inadequate flat roofs. Flats have been converted into Victorian-style terraced houses with a ground-floor front door and individual garden (Figure 2.3).

Some tall blocks of flats are now being demolished, in most cases long before they have even been paid for. In 1985 a block on the Trowbridge Estate in Hackney Wick was blown up, not for structural reasons but because the local authority policy was to remove tall blocks on social grounds (Figure 2.4). Over most of London, families with children are being moved out of the upper floors of point blocks.

> **Study question**
>
> What advice would you give to an architect designing low-cost public housing today?

On top of the problems created by bad housing has been the issue of homelessness. In 1985,

23

London

Figure 2.4 The demolition of a tower block in Hackney, 1986

25,000 people were officially registered as homeless in London, many staying in hostels or bed-and-breakfast establishments paid for by the local authority. Particularly serious is the shortage of housing for the less well-off. Not enough new houses have been built in recent years to match the growing numbers of households seeking accommodation in London.

This shortage, exacerbated by building restrictions in and beyond the strip of countryside encircling the city, known as the Green Belt, has forced prices up. The average price for a semi-detached house in London in 1987 was £81,000, compared with a figure of £43,000 for Britain as a whole. This makes it almost impossible for people living outside London to sell their house and buy an equivalent property in the capital. The whole economy is thus less efficient: people cannot move into areas offering jobs for which they might be well suited. The shortage of council (rented) housing is also severe, because of lack of investment and council house sales since 1980. Local authorities are permitted to use part of the proceeds from council-house sales to build or renovate other council houses. Unfortunately, most sales have been in outer boroughs of London, which have the best housing anyway. It is inner London boroughs which need the extra finance, but they have sold fewer properties, partly because a higher proportion of inner-London dwellings are flats.

Study question

Read the extract from Frederick Engels' book *The Condition of the Working Class in England*, published in 1845. To what extent have the problems of the nineteenth century been replaced by new types of housing problems in recent years?

Every great city has one or more slums, where the working-class is crowded together. True, poverty often dwells in hidden alleys close to the palaces of the rich; but, in general, a separate territory has been assigned to it, where, removed from the sight of the happier classes, it may struggle along as it can. These slums are pretty equally arranged in all the great towns of England, the worst houses in the worst quarters of the towns; usually one or two-storied cottages in long rows, perhaps with cellars used as dwellings, almost always irregularly built. These houses of three or four rooms and a kitchen form, throughout England, some parts of London excepted, the general dwellings of the working-class. The streets are generally unpaved, rough, dirty, filled with vegetable and animal refuse, without sewers or gutters, but supplied with foul, stagnant pools instead. Moreover, ventilation is impeded by the bad, confused method of building of the whole quarter, and since many human beings here live crowded into a small space, the atmosphere that prevails in these working-men's quarters may readily be imagined. Further, the streets serve as drying grounds in fine weather; lines are stretched across from house to house, and hung with wet clothing.

Housing tenure

Most people either own their house, rent it from a local authority, or rent it from a private landlord. This classification is known as housing tenure.

The most important change in the pattern of housing tenure in London during the period 1971–81 was a fall in the number of **households renting from private landlords** (Table 2.2). This was especially true in the inner areas, and reflected government legislation which, by controlling levels of rents and protecting the rights of tenants, made the renting of property less attractive to landlords, so that there were fewer properties available for rent. In addition, rising standards of living and recent government policy have encouraged more people to buy their own house as an alternative to renting. Only in inner west London is private renting still the most common tenure.

Despite the sale of council houses, the proportion of households **renting from the local authority** has risen in inner London. This reflects borough building programmes of the early 1970s. Council houses comprise over 50% of the total in the East End, as well as in some wards in outer London with large council estates, such as the London County Council cottage estates built at Becontree and Roehampton in the 1920s (Figure 2.5).

The highest proportion of **owner-occupied housing** is found in the outer suburbs, reflecting the predominantly middle-income family-with-children character of outer areas. Much of this housing was built by private developers between the wars.

Table 2.2 Breakdown of owner-occupiers, council tenants and private tenants, 1971 and 1981

	% of households		
	Owner occupiers	Local authority rent	Private rent
1971 Inner London	19.6	30.6	49.8
Outer London	55.8	21.0	23.2
1981 Inner London	27.3	42.8	29.9
Outer London	61.9	23.2	15.0

Study question

In many parts of inner London, pieces of land are being redeveloped. The landowners can usually make most profit by building offices or luxury flats on these sites, but such schemes are opposed by local working-class communities suffering from high levels of unemployment. Look at the extract below and answer the following questions:

1 Who are the landowners and developers of this project?
2 What is the name of the local community campaign to stop this scheme?
3 What do local people dislike about the proposed scheme, and why?

DON'T LET THEM STEAL GREENLAND DOCK !

GREENLAND DOCK SHOULD BE FOR THE PEOPLE OF SOUTHWARK. BUT INSTEAD OF ASKING PEOPLE WHAT WE WANT FIRST, THE LONDON DOCKLANDS DEVELOPMENT CORPORATION (LDDC) HAS FOISTED ON US A PLAN TO TURN GREENLAND DOCK INTO ANOTHER ST. KATHERINE'S DOCK i.e., LUXURY FLATS AND MARINAS AND NOTHING FOR US !

A massive carve up of Greenland Dock into 27 separate private development projects has been proposed by Conran Roche, consultants to the LDDC. They are only giving us until July 5th to react! We must say NO!:WE WANT A PLAN FOR THE PEOPLE; THEIR PLAN IS FOR LUXURY DEVELOPMENT :-

* 80% of all the housing is private; there is no council housing
* 60% of all housing will cost over £35,000 !
* the best sites along the river are for apartments costing over £65,000; the worst sites by the road are for "low cost" housing
* 200 yacht Marina in South Dock
* Nearly 400,000 square feet of offices - equivalent to 3 Centre Point Office Blocks !
* 900 local jobs and local community projects - Adventure Playground, Surrey Docks Farm and the Watersports Centre - are threatened !

HOMES, JOBS AND LEISURE FACILITIES FOR LOCAL PEOPLE IN GREENLAND DOCK !

STOP THE DEVELOPERS AND LDDC CARVE-UP !

FIGHT BACK WITH SOUTHWARK DOCKLANDS CAMPAIGN !

(Published by Southwark Docklands Campaign)

London

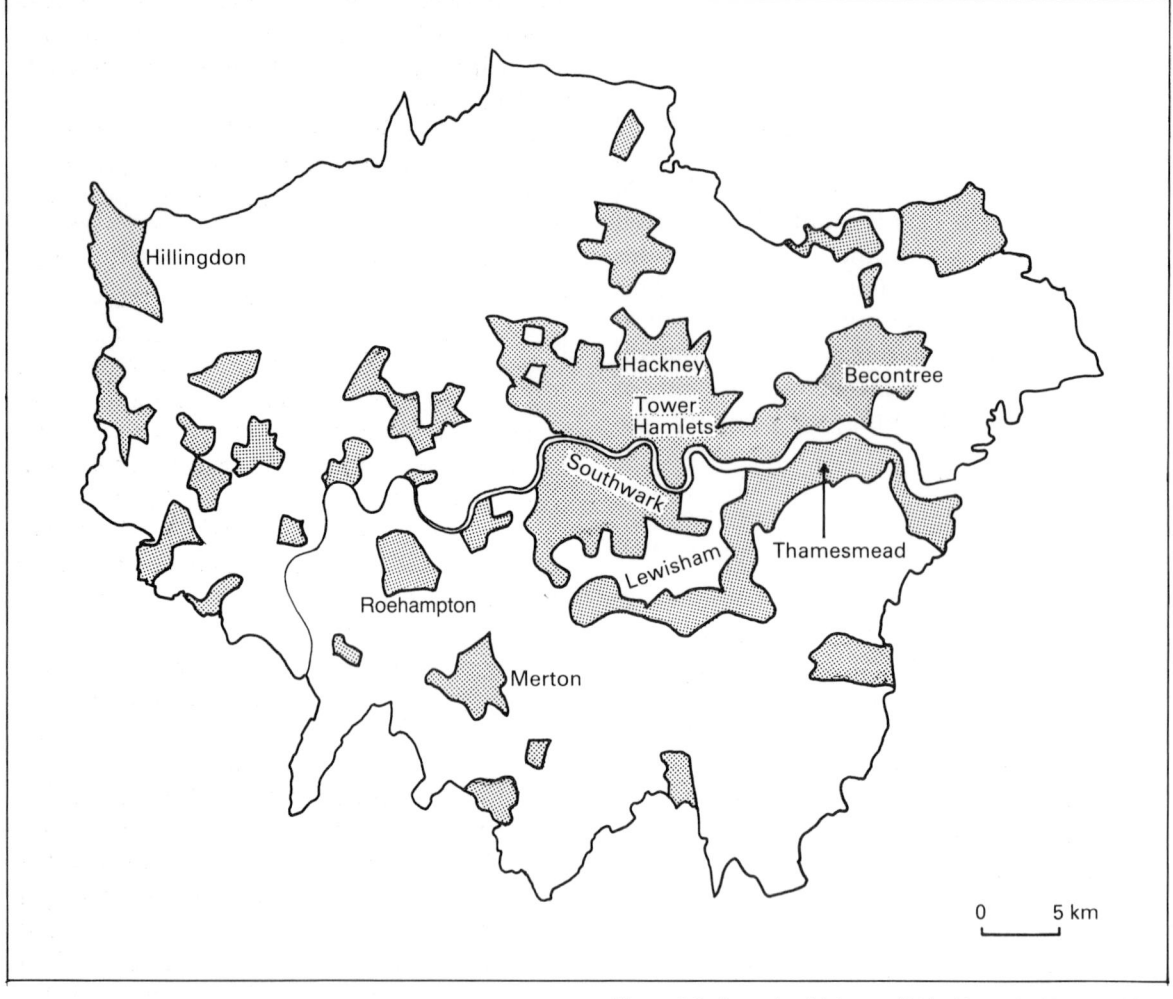

Figure 2.5 Areas in which over 40% of households rented from the local authority in 1981

Study activity

Houses can be classified in several ways:
(i) by age (e.g. pre-Victorian, Victorian, inter-war, post-war)
(ii) by tenure (owner-occupied, privately rented, council housing)
(iii) by form (detached, semi-detached, terraced, bungalows, flats)
(iv) by condition (good, average, poor)

Using these criteria, choose a small area of housing you know well and produce a map showing the distribution of different types of housing. Account for the distribution you have mapped.

Thamesmead: a low-cost housing scheme

The largest housing scheme in London in recent years has been at Thamesmead, south of the river on the eastern edge of London. It is sited on the Erith and Plumstead marshes, land which was previously used as a military testing area for the Woolwich Arsenal. The plan was produced by the Greater London Council in 1966 on the model established by British new towns. The aim of the development was to rehouse slum dwellers from inner London. With a target population of 45,000 to 48,000, it was to be completed by 1988.

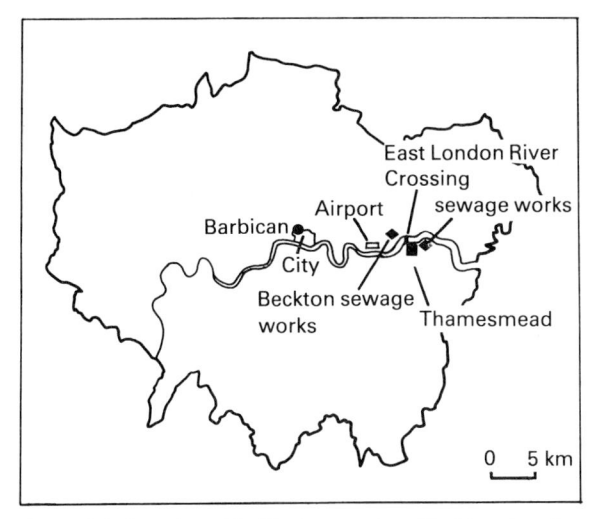

Figure 2.6 Location of the Thamesmead and Barbican housing schemes

Building the town on such a difficult site was the immediate challenge. Much of the land was marshy. Five lakes with feeder canals were constructed, both to store runoff and for recreational use. The land was also polluted with dangerous chemicals and explosives from the arsenal, and air pollution from factories, power stations and sewage works on both banks of the Thames is still a problem.

By 1985 the population had reached 20,000. Most of the people who have come to the town are white, manual workers with young families. About a third of the houses were built for sale, the remainder for rent. The rather featureless site has been successfully landscaped. Traffic is kept out of housing areas, which are grouped into neighbourhood units and served by a network of footpaths.

The town centre was not built until the late 1980s, and residents have lacked basic services. In 1985 there were only three public houses in the town. Many people shop in nearby Plumstead, making Thamesmead something of a dormitory town. The industrial estate has never taken off, and unemployment is high. The Jubilee Line, a tube link which was to connect Thamesmead with the rest of London, never materialised. Individual housing estates are very scattered, and without a clear centre the town lacks a sense of identity. Some of the more recent estates have become something of a dumping ground for problem families. Flight paths for the new airport on the opposite bank of the Thames pass over the town.

In the 1980s, cuts in government housebuilding grants to local authorities have necessitated a reduction in the planned target population to 35,000–40,000. As a result, much of the land once designated for local authority housing has been parcelled off for private development. With the abolition of the GLC, control of the town should have passed to the two boroughs within which it lies. Bexley, however, did not want the financial burden of Thamesmead to fall on its rate-payers, and Greenwich, a less wealthy borough, did not have the resources to assume responsibility. A non-profitmaking trust was therefore created to run the town.

The Barbican: a high-cost housing scheme

The Barbican development was built on a 26.5-hectare site just outside the original Roman walls of Londinium. The first bomb of the Second World War to fall in London hit the Barbican, and by 1945 much of the site was devastated.

In 1955, 11.3 hectares were set aside for offices, and today London Wall is one of the longest stretches of modern glass blocks in the city. The remaining 15.2 hectares were designated for housing by the Corporation of the City of London. Its aim was to halt the decline

Figure 2.7 Thamesmead

London

> # How to make Senior Executives happy in London
>
> At last the businessman can make his home in the City! The Barbican Residential Estate, in the very heart of London's financial area, is just a few minutes walk from the Bank of England and the Stock Exchange. Within walking distance of many of the most famous business houses, it is hardly surprising that some of the capital's most eminent business 'personalities' are choosing to make their homes there.

Figure 2.8 Advertisement for the Barbican

of population in the centre of London, something of a dead area at night and over weekends.

The Barbican residential area was designed by architects Chamberlin, Powell and Bon. They were strongly influenced by architectural ideas of the late 1950s in their use of tower blocks and concrete. One block of 43 storeys and two of 44 storeys are surrounded by terraced flats and pedestrian walkways, 2000 flats in all. The supply of open space is generous, with a school and the original church to add some character to the scheme. Roads and car parks are confined beneath the flats.

Figure 2.9 The Barbican

The housing of the Barbican was built to high standards, and its location close to the City makes it attractive to those earning high incomes and working nearby. For some, these flats are second homes, and there is a consequent loss of population at weekends. The full-time residential population is further depressed by the fact that many flats are owned by companies as accommodation for visiting executives.

1982 saw the completion of the Barbican Arts Centre, given to the nation by the City Corporation. The Centre includes two theatres, three cinemas, a concert hall, art gallery and conservatory. Costing £153 million, it took 11 years to build and used as much concrete as 19 miles of six-lane motorway. Adjoining the Centre are part of a polytechnic, a business school and a library.

The 6000 residents of the Barbican have indeed brought some life back into the City. The prices asked for the flats (£500,000 for a penthouse) reflect success of a kind. But the scheme suffers, nevertheless, from problems typical of the architectural style, and excessive use of concrete (already stained) gives the place an inhospitable feeling. It is notoriously hard to find one's way around the endless walkways and windy piazzas. There is a lack of adequate local shops, and the rigid separation of people and traffic can create a dead atmosphere. But the Barbican remains a relatively rare example of a site where the commercial logic of office development was at least partially subordinated to the social needs of the City.

> **Revision**
>
> 1 Which types of housing design create problems in London?
> 2 What factors determine the distribution of different types of housing tenure?
> 3 What is being done about bad housing in London?
> 4 What is the difference between comprehensive redevelopment and rehabilitation? Which has proved to be the more satisfactory in recent years?

3

Employment

London has always played a central role in the economy of the United Kingdom. As the major market for goods and services it has been a forcing house of change in agriculture, manufacturing and marketing, affecting the whole nation. The banking and commercial facilities which developed in London helped provide the financial backing for the agricultural and industrial revolutions which gave Britain an early lead in the world economy.

London's greatness has not, however, been as an industrial centre. In the nineteenth century, the lead sectors of textiles, iron, shipbuilding and coalmining – the basis of the Industrial Revolution in Britain – were not important in a capital which clung to more traditional industries. In the 1980s the big cities of Britain, including London, have failed to attract the growth industries such as electronics and biotechnology. Of the top ten private sector employers in London in the mid-1980s, only one – Fords at Dagenham – was a manufacturing concern.

The employment structure of London is, therefore, dominated by the administrative and service sectors. The largest employers in 1986 were the borough councils (260,000 jobs), the Health Service (140,000), central government civil service (130,000), banks and retailers.

The 1980s saw unemployment rising in all parts of London. In 1986, when the overall UK unemployment rate stood at 13.4% the average for London was 10.6%. But this average concealed considerable variations within the capital, many inner-city areas having rates of over 20%. Between 1980 and 1984 there was an annual net loss of 31,000 jobs from London.

> **Study activity**
>
> Draw a bar graph to summarise the employment structure of London in 1981 (Table 3.1). Why are services so much more important than manufacturing in terms of jobs?

Table 3.1 London employment breakdown by sector, 1981

Services	
Professional and scientific (mainly office jobs)	570,000
Insurance, banking, finance (mainly office jobs)	463,000
Public administration (mainly office jobs)	314,000
Distribution (inc. retail)	477,000
Transport and communications	374,000
Construction	162,000
Gas, electricity, water	45,000
Other (inc. tourism)	450,000
Total	2,855,000

Manufacturing	
Paper, printing, publishing	118,000
Electrical engineering	115,000
Food, drink and tobacco	69,000
Mechanical engineering	68,000
Metal goods	45,000
Chemicals	45,000
Clothing and footwear	31,000
Other	159,000
Total	650,000

> **Study question**
>
> Describe and explain the pattern of high unemployment shown in Figure 3.1.

London

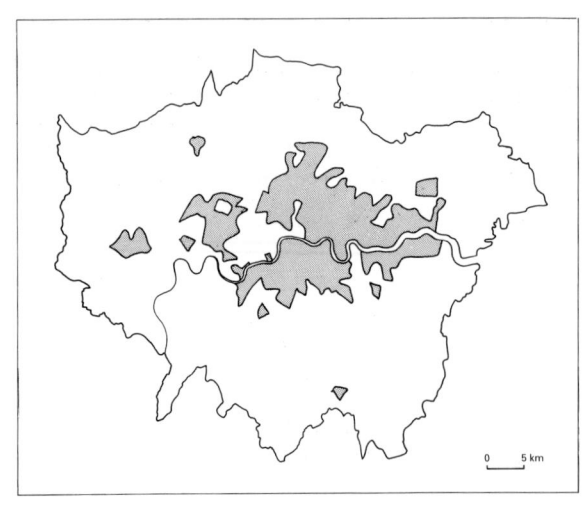

Figure 3.1 Areas where over 15% of the population were unemployed in 1985

Offices

In terms of office jobs, the country is dominated by London. Fourteen per cent of office jobs in England and Wales are found in just two areas of London – the City and the West End.

Individual parts of London contain concentrations of particular types of office (Table 3.2), some clustering around lead institutions (e.g. stockbrokers around the Stock Exchange), others choosing sites for reasons of prestige and access to clients. In general, while office districts in the City are clearly defined, those in the West End are not. The City is dominated by financial institutions. The West End contains a mixture of offices, locating here for reasons of prestige and access to staff: headquarters of large companies, advertising agents, television and cinema organisations, air transport companies.

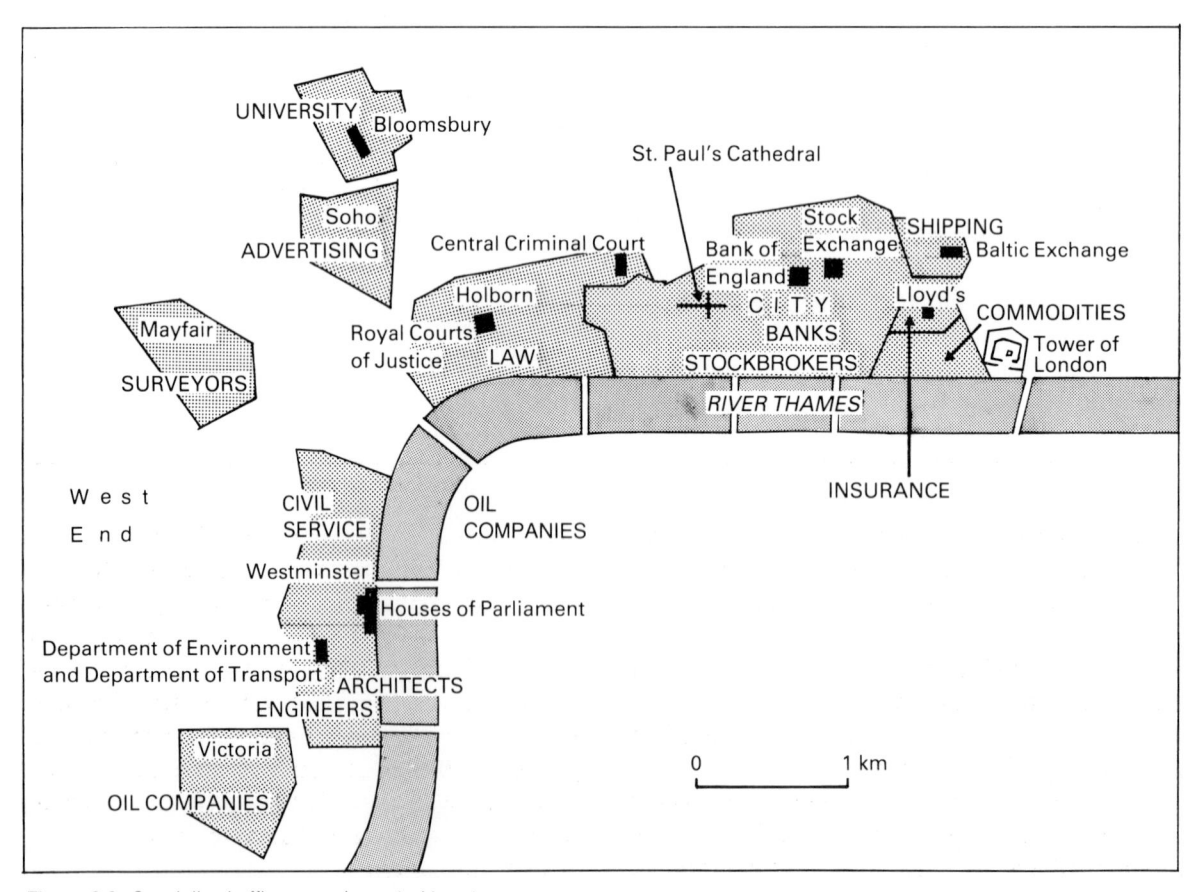

Figure 3.2 Specialised office areas in central London

Table 3.2 Specialised office areas in London

Function	Location	Trend, 1980–87	Function	Location	Trend, 1980–87
Banks	The City around the Bank of England	Some foreign banks have been forced into sites on the City fringes because of a lack of large available premises in the City	Newspaper publishers	Around Fleet Street	Moving out to dockland
			Civil service	Whitehall, near to Parliament	Decentralisation of less important office jobs
Insurance	Around Lloyd's in the east of the City	Some insurance companies have moved outside central London altogether.	Barristers	Fleet Street and the Temple, based in the four Inns (groups of chambers), near to the Old Bailey and Royal Courts of Justice	
Stockbrokers and jobbers	North of the Stock Exchange in the City	Some movement within the City as they joined merchant banks to form financial supermarkets in the mid-1980s	University of London	Main offices in Bloomsbury	
			Oil companies	Victoria	
			Surveyors	Mayfair	
Shipping companies	Eastern side of the City close to the Baltic Exchange	Some movement to cheaper City fringes	Solicitors	Holborn, close to the barristers	
			Advertising	Soho	
Commodity brokers	Near Tower of London in the City, close to the Baltic Exchange (grain), Metal Exchange (hard commodities) and Commodity Exchange (soft commodities)		Engineers, architects	Westminster, near Department of the Environment	

The City has a number of advantages as an office centre. Ringed by railway termini, it is easily accessible to commuters. Location in the City carries a certain prestige. The proximity of related offices enables people to do business on a face-to-face basis. Because market conditions are constantly changing and contracts need to be settled quickly, much trade is still done by people meeting personally. Individual firms are linked to certain key institutions and need to be within walking distance of them: for example, banks concentrate around the Bank of England, and insurance brokers around Lloyd's.

The City has always been the heart of the financial sector. Financial services originated here to administer trade based on the port of London. In the seventeenth and eighteenth centuries traders met in coffee houses near the port. Individual coffee houses came to specialise in particular lines of business: commodities, insurance, shipping or banking. Eventually, the men who gathered in these centres set up the institutions we know today.

London

Property booms

Central London saw office building booms in the early 1960s, early 1970s, and 1980s (Table 3.3). In every case, controversy and conflict accompanied the boom.

During the Second World War one third of the City was devastated, creating 91 hectares of land with potential for development. Reconstruction was delayed by a shortage of materials after the war, but by 1959 9 million square feet of office space had been built.

The New Lloyds of London

Table 3.3 Office building in London

Date	Event	Boom/Slump
1960	Office development permit 1964–78 (controlling office growth in London)	BOOM 1958–64 — Shell Buildings, Millbank Tower
	Civic Amenities Act 1967 (Conservation Areas)	SLUMP 1964–71
1970	Skeffington Report 1969 (recommending greater public participation in the planning process)	
	controversy 1971–78	BOOM 1971–74 — Nat West Tower, Stock Exchange
	Location of Offices Bureau wound up, 1978	SLUMP 1974–80
1980	Coin Street controversy 1974–84	BOOM 1980–88
	Green Giant at Vauxhall Cross rejected, 1981	
	Prince Charles opposes National Gallery extension, 1984	Broadgate
	Palumbo's plan for a Mies van der Rohe building in the City rejected, 1985	New Lloyd's, London Bridge City, Canary Wharf
	Office developments in dockland encouraged by LDDC and Enterprise Zone	

The peak of the first property boom came around 1963. Finance was available, and prices were rising. New building techniques and architectural styles produced a number of tall steel and glass towers. London County Council planners contrived to place taller buildings at important traffic junctions and alongside major open spaces. This discouraged developments which obscured historic silhouettes. The tallest blocks were not, therefore, built in the City of London. They sprang up in odd places all over the centre, such as the Shell Tower by Waterloo Bridge and Millbank Tower on the Embankment.

In some cases good buildings were lost to make way for office schemes, such as the Euston Arch, demolished in 1961 despite opposition from the Victorian Society. The public came to resent the vast fortunes being made by property developers, especially after a number of corrupt practices came to light.

Legislation passed by a Labour administration meant that virtually no more planning consents for office buildings were granted in the city centre between 1964 and 1971. During this period demand for office space exceeded supply, so when the legislation was amended in 1971, the building boom resumed. In the 1970s, 9.4 million square feet of office space was built in the City alone, including the National Westminster Tower and the new Stock Exchange. In 1974 the property market crashed, and building slowed down until 1980. The designation of **Conservation Areas** also restricted scope for redevelopment.

Figure 3.3 Covent Garden before and after the closure of the fruit and vegetable market

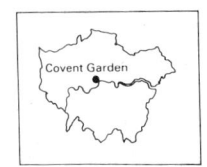

Conflict at Covent Garden. From 1654 to 1974 the main wholesale fruit, vegetable and flower market for London was a cramped site at Covent Garden. In 1966 the decision was made to move the market out within the next ten years. Once abandoned, the market site represented a marvellous opportunity for redevelopment. In 1968 a draft plan was produced by the GLC, City of Westminster and Borough of Camden. The plan proposed to redevelop 22 of the 38 hectares, including the demolition of half the houses in the area. Private developers were to be invited to build offices, an international conference centre, a large hotel and new shops. Had this plan been implemented, it would have destroyed the character of the area.

1968, however, was a watershed year in the history of comprehensive redevelopment. It was

London

the end of the 1960s property boom. Londoners were becoming disillusioned with post-war urban motorways, characterless office blocks and high-rise flats. In 1969 the Skeffington Report proposed that local plans should be put before a public inquiry before implementation. At this inquiry the Covent Garden Community Association opposed the plan, attracting sympathy from the media and Londoners generally. The plan was finally wrecked when, in 1973, 250 buildings in the area were **listed** (given official government protection), in addition to 40 that were already protected from demolition. Two Conservation Areas were also created.

> **Study questions**
>
> Who stood to gain and who to lose from the plan to redevelop the Covent Garden market as an office district?

In 1974 a new plan was put forward, and approved, with modification, in 1978. The market buildings have been renovated, occupied by shops and restaurants, and the area has since become popular with tourists and visitors to the West End. Low-rise houses have been built for local people, and through-traffic is restricted. Small industrial and craft workshops have been encouraged. Any development likely to detract from the appearance of the area has been opposed.

But while the physical character of the area has been preserved, the original community has not. Property values have risen rapidly, and traditional firms are disappearing as their leases expire. As the original tenants die, their houses are renovated by private landlords and leased at higher rents to a different class of people. Gradually, the character of 'the Garden' is changing.

Many other office schemes have resulted in conflicts between developers and local residents. In the 1970s, a series of public inquiries was held to decide the future of the Coin Street site by the National Theatre (Figure 3.4). The architect Richard Rogers produced a scheme costing £150 million for one million square feet of offices on the site, with blocks up to 14 storeys high. This was opposed by the GLC and local

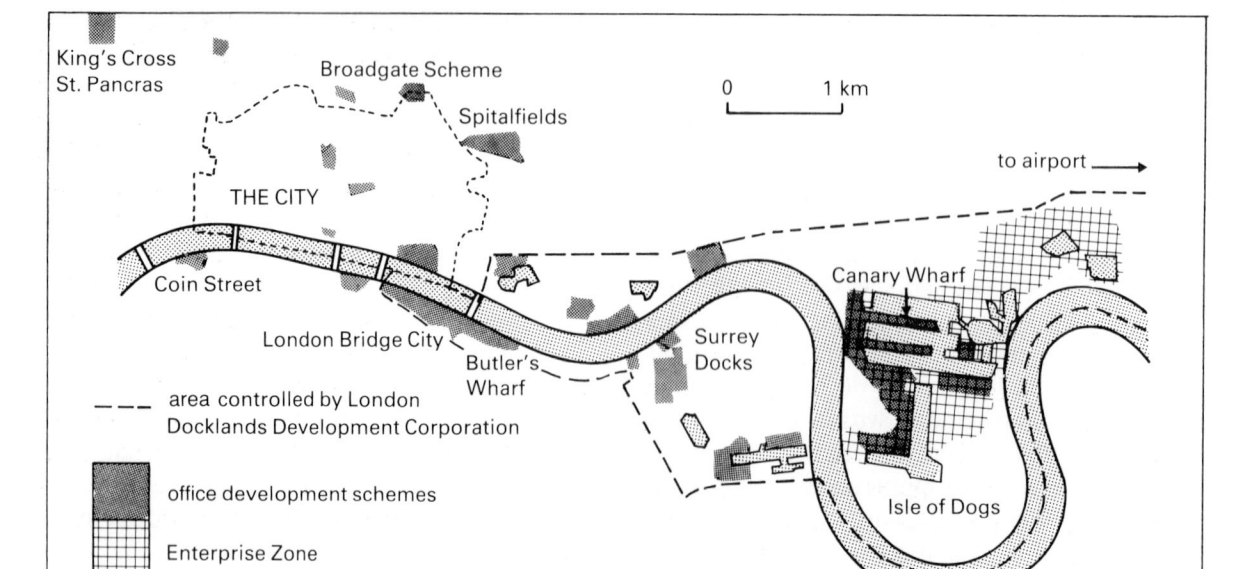

Figure 3.4 Office developments in the City and Dockland, mid-1980s.

people, who wanted houses they could afford and jobs appropriate to their skills. In 1984 the GLC bought the land for £3 million, and their £30 million scheme will produce 400 dwellings, 126,000 square footage of studio workshops, and 0.6 hectares of open parkland.

The 1980s have again seen an office building boom in the city. The adoption of computers, word processors and other pieces of information technology has meant that many office blocks, some built as recently as the 1960s, are structurally inadequate. To lay the necessary cables, larger spaces are needed in the gap between ceilings and the floors above. Air conditioning has also become a basic requirement. A second important change has been a recent demand from many firms for very large open-plan dealing floors. This has arisen as a result of the deregulation of the City in 1986, known as **Big Bang**. Changes in the Stock Exchange rules have encouraged competition between City institutions and generated a rise in turnover. For this reason, they need larger dealing rooms

A related development was the decision to allow foreign firms to join the Stock Exchange. Many foreign financial conglomerates are able to offer a wide range of services to the customer under one roof: banking, money-dealing, broking, jobbing and insurance. Individual British firms have traditionally concerned themselves with just one of these activities. In order to deal with the new challenge, British companies have formed partnerships: the merchant bank Warburgs, for example, is grouping with brokers Rowe and Pitman, jobbers Ackroyd and Smithers and gilt-edged brokers Mullens. These new **financial supermarkets** will be able to do more dealing on world securities markets than before, and they again require large open-plan dealing rooms. Uninterrupted spaces allow individuals to exchange market information more easily, and permit more flexible use of the technological hardware.

The arrival of the foreign securities houses in London has also pushed up demand for office space. By virtue of its position in the time zones, London is ideally placed as a centre for trade with other parts of the world. Foreign institutions are now arriving from Japan, America, Europe and the Middle and Far East.

Current demand, therefore, is for new office space, and particularly for low-rise office buildings with large dealing floors. Over 70% of banks who took space in the City in 1985 took in excess of 10,000 square feet. Between 1980 and 1985, 8.6 million square feet of office space was built in the City, almost as much in five years as in the whole of any previous decade.

Much of London's new building is taking place within the City itself. Stanhope Securities are building 1.25 million square feet of offices adjacent to Liverpool Street Station – the £300 million Broadgate scheme (Figure 3.4). However, there are constraints upon the total amount of new City office space. Fragmented leaseholds mean that few large sites are available. Large numbers of buildings are protected under the 1967 Civil Amenities Act, and the City Corporation's 1986 plan restricts further development in all but a third of the 'Square Mile'. In 1985, plans to demolish an area west of the Bank of England and build a glass tower designed by Mies van der Rohe were rejected by the Secretary of State.

Pressure of demand has therefore generated an unprecedented number of office development schemes in the City fringes – areas around the edge of the City. East of Liverpool Street station, the Spitalfields area is gradually being transformed. In 1982 Central and City Properties completed a £12 million warehouse conversion at Bishops Court, creating 68,000 square feet of floorspace. The Spitalfields fruit and vegetable market is being converted into a Covent Garden-style covered shopping centre, further increasing pressure in the area. The 100-acre site north of King's Cross and St. Pancras railway stations, a vast area of old sidings, warehouses and industry, is to be redeveloped in the 1990s as offices, leisure facilities and a business park. All these sites have the advantage of lower rents, falling from £30 per square foot per annum in the centre to £15 per square foot on the City fringes in 1987.

Between Tower Bridge and London Bridge on the south bank, 2.2 million square feet of

Figure 3.5. Barge House Street: inter-war warehouses being converted to offices

offices are being built on the site of Hay's Wharf. This scheme, costing £350 million, is financed by the Kuwaiti royal family and managed by St Martin's Property Corporation. It will incorporate a private hospital, shops and light industrial units. The first phase of the scheme, known as London Bridge City, was completed in 1986.

East of Tower Bridge, 5 hectares of derelict warehouses are being developed in a £30-million scheme backed by Sir Terence Conran. Here, we will see offices, shops, a hotel, flats, workshops and a museum. All over dockland, these and other sites are being developed at a pace which has not been seen since the building boom of the 1960s.

Many recent office schemes have been opposed by Labour-controlled local authorities, and local people. Most of the key sites along the river are, however, controlled by the London Docklands Development Corporation. Public inquiries are not required: permission for development is obtained by the LDDC direct from the Environment Secretary. The Butler's Wharf Scheme (Figure 3.4), for example, went ahead in the face of opposition from the North Southwark Community Development Group, who wanted jobs for the local unemployed and 2000 homes.

Decentralisation from central London

From 1964 to 1979, the government required any office development scheme in London above a certain fixed floorspace threshold to obtain an **Office Development Permit**. It was hoped that offices refused such a permit would move to the assisted areas, where unemployment was high. The scheme was administered by the **Location of Offices Bureau**, which also mounted an advertising campaign stressing the disadvantages of a London location (Figure 3.6.). Between 1963 and 1976 the LOB moved 150,000 office jobs out of central London. Another 150,000 are believed to have moved

Figure 3.6. Advertisement put out by the Location of Offices Bureau

Employment

without contacting the LOB. The government also moved some 30,000 of its own administrative staff to the regions. The Driver and Vehicle Licensing Centre, and the Land Registry, for example, both moved to Swansea.

Other forces have been at work to encourage decentralisation. Rates and rents in central areas are three to five times those of outer areas. Costs of commuting have risen. Many older office blocks have become obsolete. Some London local authorities, as well as the GLC, deliberately restricted office development in favour of houses, services and jobs for local people.

The 1969 **Greater London Development Plan** designated sites for office centres in Croydon, Ilford, Kingston and Wood Green, all in the outer suburbs. Croydon was, in fact, already becoming an important office centre by this time. The Croydon Corporation Act 1956 had given the Corporation power to buy 0.8 hectares of land in the centre of the town. When the 1960s office boom began, this site was enthusiastically developed by the Corporation as an office district which today employs over 30,000 people.

Eighty per cent of office development outside the centre has taken place in the southern and western suburbs (Figure 3.7). Proximity to

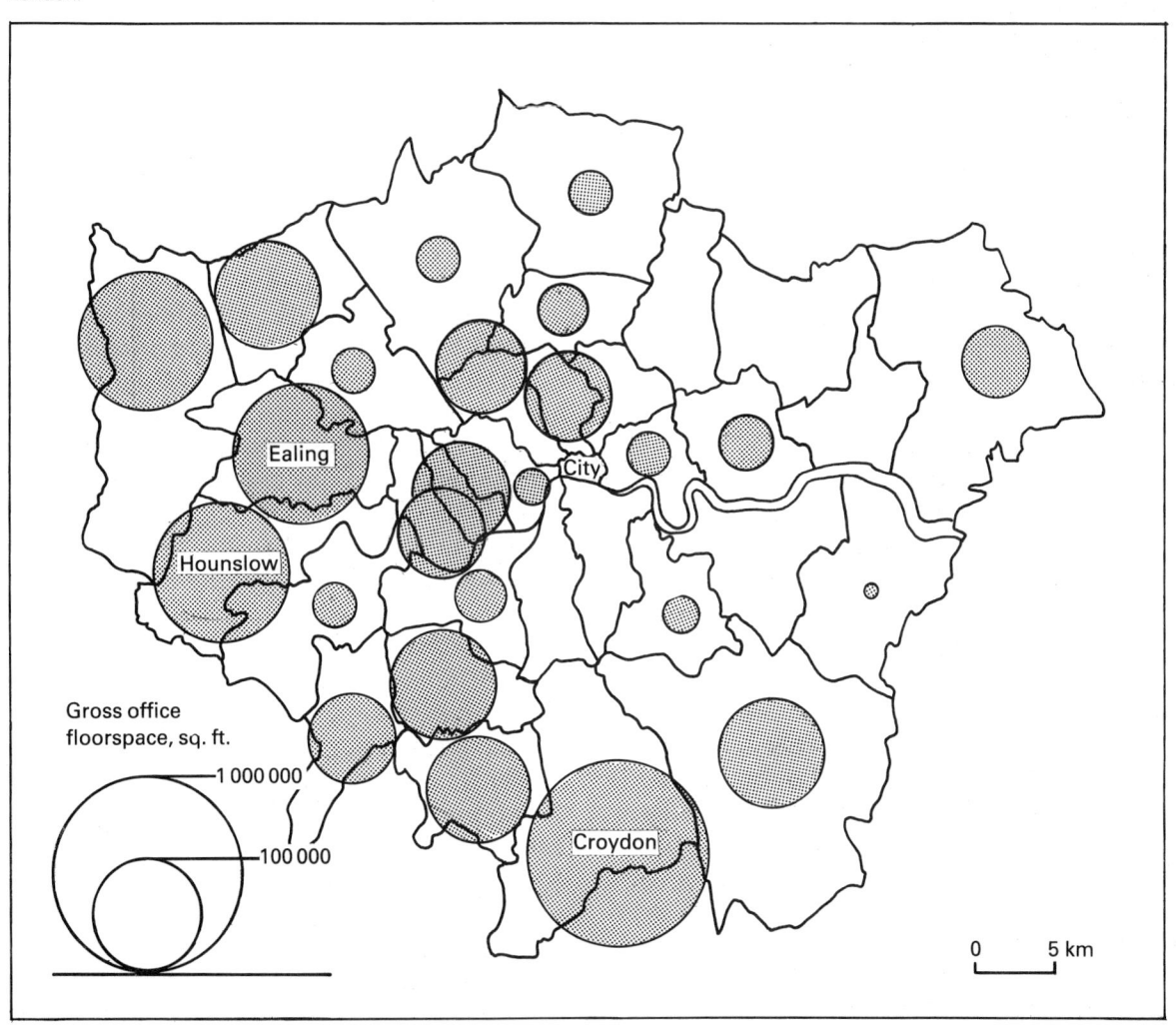

Figure 3.7 Office developments exceeding 10,000 square feet of floorspace, built in the period 1984–1985, outside the City of London.

Heathrow Airport, the M4 and M3 has helped. In 1984–86 the fastest growth was in Ealing and Hammersmith.

Since 1970 some offices have moved out of London altogether. Towns along the Western Corridor, such as Windsor, Slough, Maidenhead, Reading, Newbury and Basingstoke, have successfully developed as office centres. Two types of business have been particularly prone to decentralisation: major manufacturing firms and insurance companies. Firms moving out of central London in the late 1970s included W.H. Smith, Blue Circle, Chemical Bank and Commercial Union.

The scale of office decentralisation is, however, exaggerated. Since 1979 the rate of office loss from London has been half that of the period 1964–78. Some big firms *have* decentralised, but at the same time many smaller firms moved *into* London and expanded there.

> **Study question**
>
> Planning between 1944 and 1978 concentrated on moving people and jobs out of London. Was this policy wise in view of the problems of unemployment in London today?

One of the most important influences on the supply of offices is the role of the financial institutions. These are the people whose business it is to invest the money of others: merchant banks, insurance companies and pension funds, for example. Most offices built in London are paid for by such organisations. Offices represent a good investment because in recent years property values have risen steadily, and the owner of the building also receives regular rent from the tenants. The institutions were spending around £2 billion each year on property in the UK in the late 1980s. Many individual office blocks in the City cost over £100 million.

One of the roles of these institutional investors is to reinforce the existing concentration of offices in the centre of London. The investors require two things above all else – a high rental income and a safe investment. Both these requirements are met by offices in central areas. Investing outside established office concentrations is much less attractive.

Retailing

The relocation of wholesaling

Wholesale markets have existed in central London since the Roman forum was built close to present-day Leadenhall. The Anglo-Saxon word for market was 'ceap', and by late Saxon times two large markets were established in the City – Westcheap (today's Cheapside) and Eastcheap (still the name given to this eastern area of the City). Individual streets specialised in the sale of particular products, and this is reflected in street names today – Cornhill, Poultry, Bread Street, Wood Street, Haymarket, etc.

Some wholesale markets remain in central London (Figure 3.8), but most have closed or moved out of the central area. New markets have been built in the suburbs, such as the Western International fruit and vegetable market off the M4 near Junction 3.

In 1974 the Covent Garden fruit, vegetable and flower market moved to a site at Nine Elms in Vauxhall (Figure 3.9). The Covent Garden site had become too congested for modern lorries. Local residents suffered from early morning noise and the mess made by the market, and there was a good deal of pilfering from insecure storage areas. The new 28-hectare site was formerly a railway goods yard. The original intention was to build a new line into the market and bring goods in by rail. In the event, British Rail backed out of the scheme and so the market is served by lorries, 800–1000 each day. With a trading space of 400,000 square feet and 1985 sales of over £250 million, the new market is a success. It employs over 3000, and there is space for 2000 commercial vehicles and 1000 cars. Around 180,000 square feet of office space was built to administer the market and, with its perimeter wall and closed-circuit TV system, the area is secure.

In 1982 the Billingsgate fish market moved from its old site near the centre of London to the Isle of Dogs (Figure 3.8). It had been at its orig-

Employment

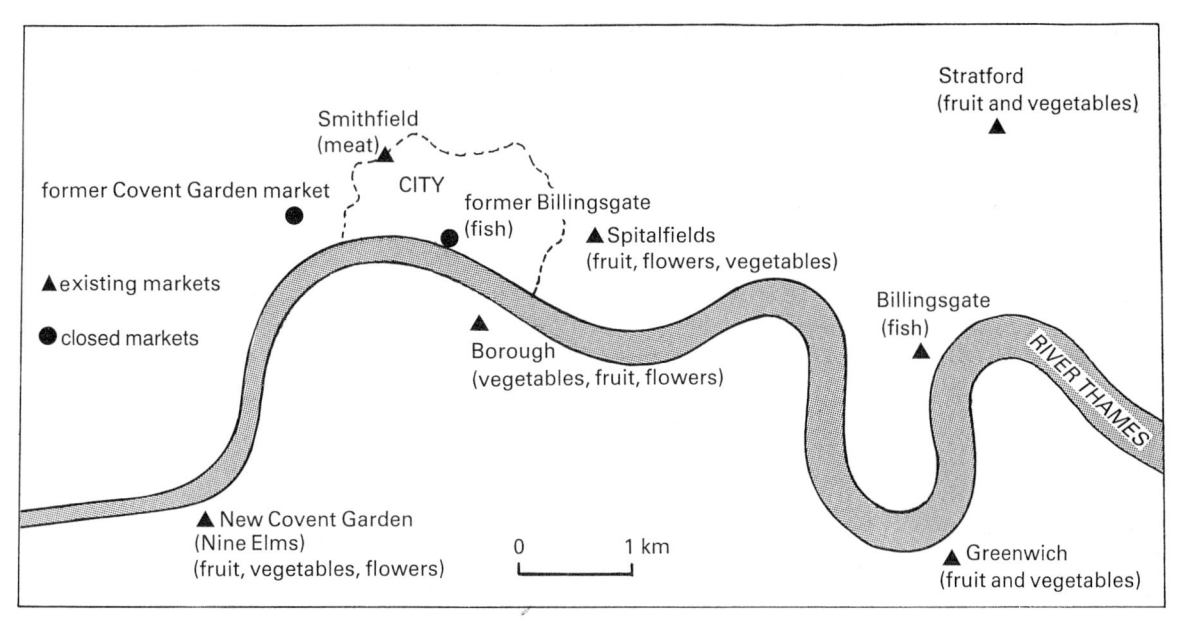

Figure 3.8 Wholesale markets in central London.

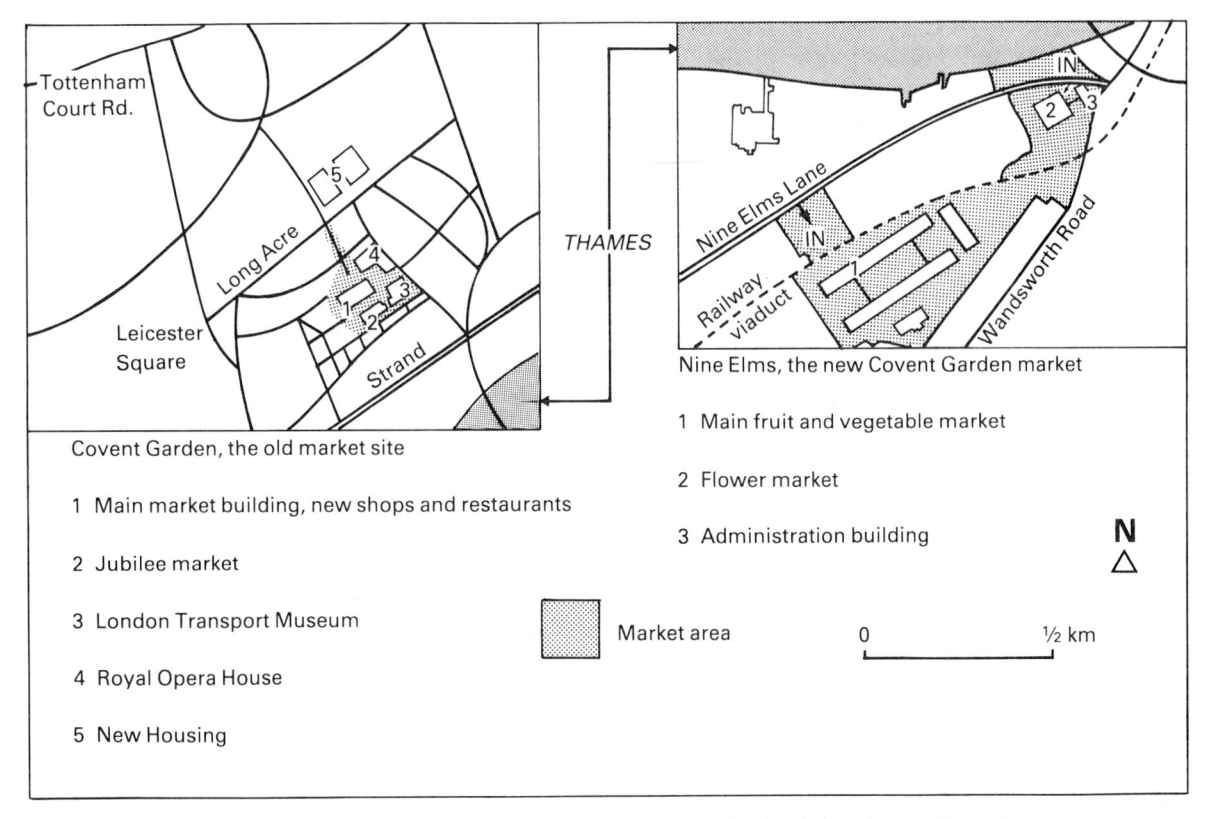

Figure 3.9 The parts of London occupied by the present and former Covent Garden fruit and vegetable market

39

London

inal site, by the Thames on the southern side of the City, since Roman times. As with Covent Garden market, the buildings and lorry park had become too small and congested. The old market became a listed building, and was converted into offices. The new fish market in the docks cost £11 million, partly financed by government inner-city renewal aid. Its easterly location was an improvement, because most of the lorries carrying fish come in from the east coast, and many of the porters live in the East End. The large 5-hectare site includes parking space for 600 vehicles.

Street markets

Although the number of **street markets** has declined since 1920, they are still an important branch of retailing in working-class areas of London (see Figure 3.10). Street market stalls are preferred by casual traders and those who cannot afford to buy a shop. Some street markets operate in the outer suburbs, at Romford and Bromley for example, but most are found in inner areas. Some specialise in one commodity, such as the antiques market in Portobello Road on Saturdays.

Shopping centres

Shopping centres in London form a **hierarchy**, from large centres such as Kingston and Lewisham, serving over 100,000 people, down to the smallest corner shops. Large centres have a higher proportion of big stores, supermarkets and non-food shops. Relatively few large centres are found in north London, which has better access to the city centre, and in east London, where average incomes are lower.

The shopping hierarchy is dominated by the West End, which serves customers from all over London and surrounding regions, as well as tourists. Areas within the West End specialise in particular products: King's Road and Carnaby Street in fashion clothes, Bond Street in antiques and jewellery, Savile Row and Jermyn Street in men's clothing.

Many big shopping centres have increased their attractiveness in recent years by improving the shopping environment. Streets such as Carnaby Street have become **pedestrianised**. **Covered shopping malls** have been built in Lewisham, Wood Green, Wandsworth and many other high streets (Figure 3.11).

The construction of **supermarkets**, **chain stores** and **discount warehouses** in the larger centres has reduced the number of customers using smaller shopping centres. More people own cars, fridges and deep freezers and prefer to make one big shopping trip to a centre with a wide range of shops rather than many small trips to local shops. The local, independent

Figure 3.10 Location of street markets in London, 1985

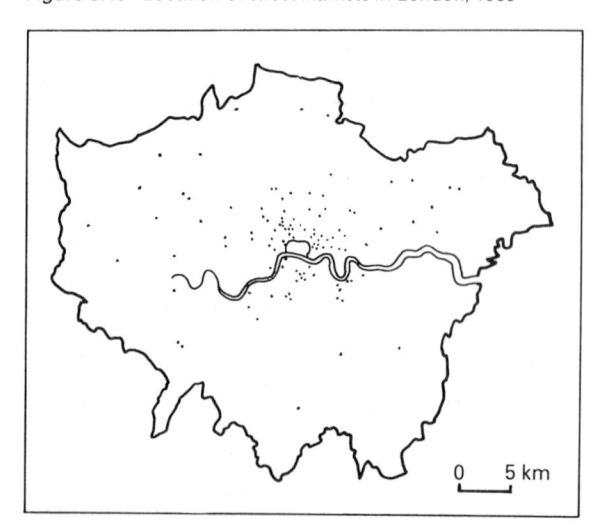

Figure 3.11 Four of the major covered shopping malls in London

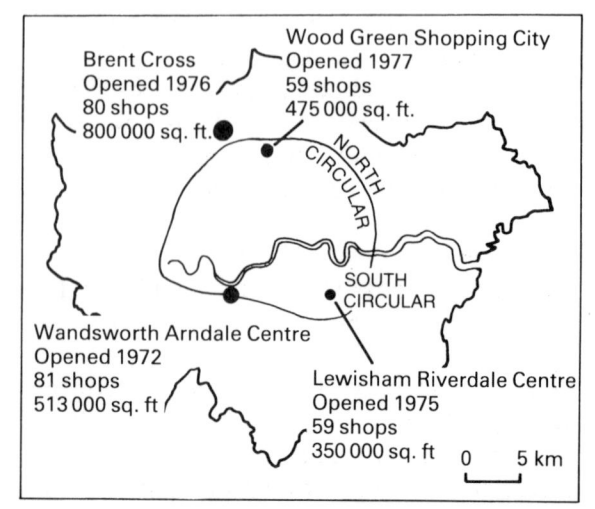

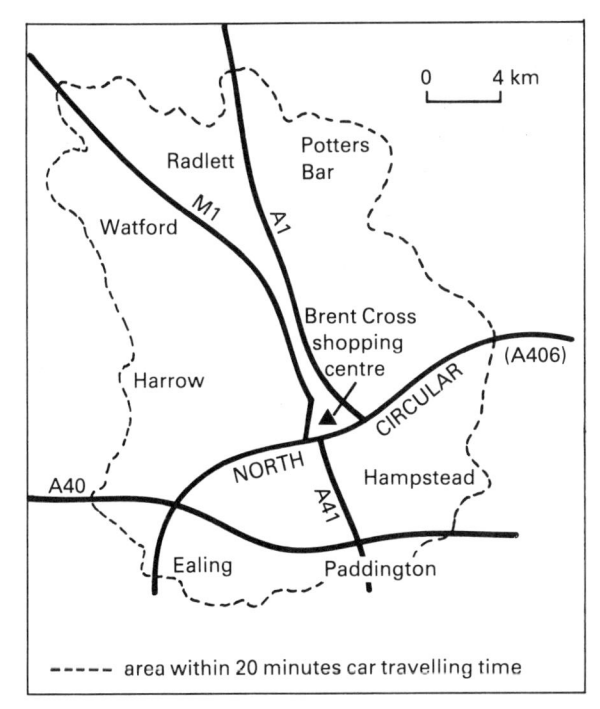

Location of Brent Cross shopping centre

retailers, unable to compete with the prices of supermarkets, have suffered as a result.

Another important trend in the future might be the construction of large covered shopping centres on the edge of London. The only major development of this type so far is at Brent Cross in north-west London, which opened in 1976 (Figure 3.11). The centre occupies a 21-hectare site bounded by major trunk roads, the North Circular and M1 motorway extension. Over 78% of shoppers come by car, and there is parking for 4500 vehicles. The centre is also well served by bus and underground services. There are two major 'anchor' stores (John Lewis and Fenwicks), four other multiple retailers and 90 smaller shops. The centre is open until 8 p.m. Monday to Friday, 6 p.m. on Saturdays. With the completion of the M25 orbital motorway, several companies have applied to build similar shopping centres around the periphery of London.

These trends are altering the pattern of retailing in London. People are now travelling further to shops as large centres grow at the expense of small parades, and as out-of-town developments reduce trade in suburban shops. Those with cars and jobs gain from the greater choice and longer opening hours. The old, the unemployed, and families without a car find that the standard of local provision, on which they depend, is declining.

Study question

How do you think trends in retailing will affect the number, types and location of shops over the next 30 years?

Tourism and recreation

Just under 25 million tourists visited London in 1985, a 47% increase since 1975 (Table 3.4). Rising standards of living, the shorter working week, longer holidays, cheaper, faster travel and the organisation of tourist facilities have combined to increase the number of visitors to the capital. In 1985 tourists spent £3 billion in central London. The tourist sector employed 230,000 Londoners, and an additional 150,000 in related jobs – 10% of London's workforce.

The most obvious manifestation of the tourist boom has been an increase in the number of hotels. The 1969 **Development of Tourism Act** initiated grants to help increase the volume of tourist accommodation. Most of these new hotels are in west London, especially Kensington and Earls Court, as well as close to the airports at Heathrow and Gatwick.

The benefits of tourism are not as great as they might seem. Most tourists visit only a small

Table 3.4 Tourism Statistics

Number of visitors to London (millions)	1975	1980	1985
Overseas	7	7.5	9
Domestic	10	13	14

West End theatres	1980	1985
No. of theatres	36	43
Box-office revenue	£45m	£90m

London

number of places, mostly in central London, and demand is seasonal. Those working in the tourist sector are generally badly paid and work unsocial hours. A quarter of tourist jobs are only part-time. A high proportion of tourist spending ends up in the hands of tour operators and does not directly help the capital. Tourist buses and coaches are a major traffic obstacle in summer months, especially around the most popular attractions where parking facilities are limited.

Leisure, on the other hand, is one of the very few areas where large numbers of new jobs could be created. The industry is growing rapidly as a result of the increased amounts of leisure time at the population's disposal, high unemployment and the increasing emphasis on part-time work and job-sharing schemes. Increasing numbers of tourists are visiting as international travel becomes easier, the environment of tourist London is improved and exchange rates move in favour of the UK. Many jobs in the leisure industry are low skilled, but this may be an advantage as most of the unemployed in inner London *are* unskilled. In the period 1985–1990, leisure jobs are expected to grow at a rate of 2.4% per annum in Great Britain as a whole, faster than any other sector.

In London, over 1700 hectares (10.7% of total land area) is public open space (Figure 3.13). Many of London's oldest parks were originally protected from development because they were **Crown land**. Hyde Park was a piece of hunting land landscaped by William III to provide a handsome setting for Kensington Palace. The 810 hectares of Richmond Park were purchased by Charles I for use as royal hunting park; 600 deer remain there today. Greenwich Park was first used as a royal park in the fifteenth century, and was walled in by James I in 1619.

Some parks originated as **common land**. Such was the case with Hampstead Heath. In the mid-nineteenth century the lord of the manor tried to enclose and develop the land, but local people restricted him, preserving their commoners' rights until the heath was purchased by the Metropolitan Board of Works in 1870.

More recent parks were created specifically to provide areas of recreation. In 1840 the government purchased 80 hectares of land in the East End and created Victoria Park. Similarly, in 1966 the 19 kilometre long Lea Valley Regional Park was created along the Lea Navigation, a sequence of open spaces with provision for sailing, cycling, horse riding and golf (Figure 3.13). Since 1980, large parts of dockland have been converted for recreational use, particularly for water sports.

However, even in the field of recreational activity, community conflicts can arise. A good example of this is provided by Battersea Power Station. This was closed in 1983, but could not be demolished because it is a listed building. The Central Electricity Generating Board held a competition to decide its future, and this was won by the Roche and Company Consortium, who own Alton Towers theme park. Their plan was to turn the one million square feet of space available into an indoor theme park with restaurants, shops, cinemas, an ice lake, balloon rides, discotheque and other amusements. The scheme was priced at £60 million, and may attract an estimated four million visitors each year. Many of these would come by car, and a car park was to be provided on the adjacent South Lambeth goods yard site. It was estimated that the first phase would be completed by 1988, the second by 1990. It would generate 4500 new jobs on the site and about 2000 others in related services.

In 1986 Wandsworth, the local authority concerned, gave approval on certain conditions. A new railway station was to be built to minimise the number of people needing to come by car. The theme park was to recruit mainly *local*

Figure 3.12 Battersea power station

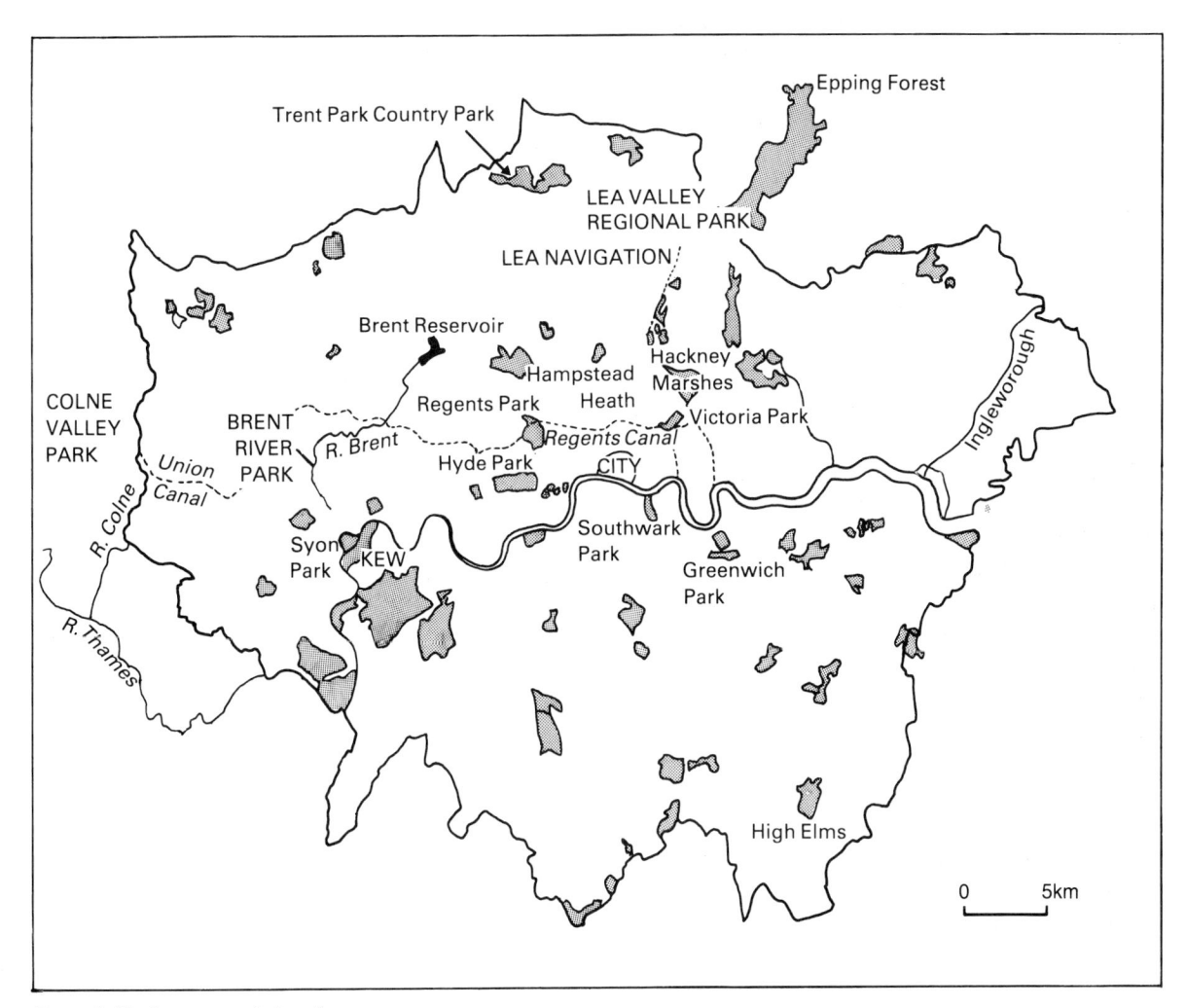

Figure 3.13 Open space in London

people into the jobs, and these employees were to be given proper training so that they learnt useful skills.

There was some opposition to the development amongst local people. Wealthier residents were worried about losing the small amount of on-street parking available near the power station, and about congestion on the nearby bridges and at Vauxhall. The majority of local people, however, are council tenants. They were more concerned about the high level of unemployment in Wandsworth, and did not believe that the theme park was the best way to provide the jobs they need. They founded the Battersea Power Station Community Group to oppose it. Their argument was that it was improbable that 4500 jobs would be created, and they felt that most of the new jobs that did materialise would be unskilled, poorly paid and seasonal. As an alternative, they put forward a scheme to divide the power station between a leisure centre, conference centre and industrial workshops. On the goods yard site, further workshops and houses would be built. This scheme, however, inevitably required some public funding, and has not been pursued. The original leisure park project is now under way.

> **Study question**
>
> Why do tourist developments so often result in conflicts of land use?

London

Many Londoners, of course, go for recreation beyond the built-up area of London itself. An early example is provided by the remarkable **plotland developments**. Between 1919 and 1947 many less well-off Londoners bought small plots of farmland near to London on which they built their own holiday and weekend homes. The land they bought was usually cheap because it was of marginal value to the farmer: sites which were liable to flood along the banks of the Thames or River Lea, or dry upland sites along the North Downs (Figure 3.14). Farmers made money from the sales, and the plots satisfied a growing demand for holidays in the countryside. Many of the little houses that resulted were built by the plot owners, and were badly constructed as a result. They can still be seen today.

Manufacturing industry

Half a million people worked in manufacturing industry in London in 1986, one seventh of the capital's workforce. This represents a massive decline since 1951 (1.5m jobs), or even 1971 (1.0m). The impact of this decline has been uneven, depending on the types of industry dominant in different parts of the city.

Many of the oldest industries in London are found **along the Thames** (Figure 3.15). They were based on sea-borne trade: timber, sugar, grain, and other commodities imported from the Empire to be processed near the docks. Only a few of these industries survive today – such as the Tate and Lyle sugar refinery, an important local employer in the East End. Further down

Figure 3.14 Plotland developments in south-east England

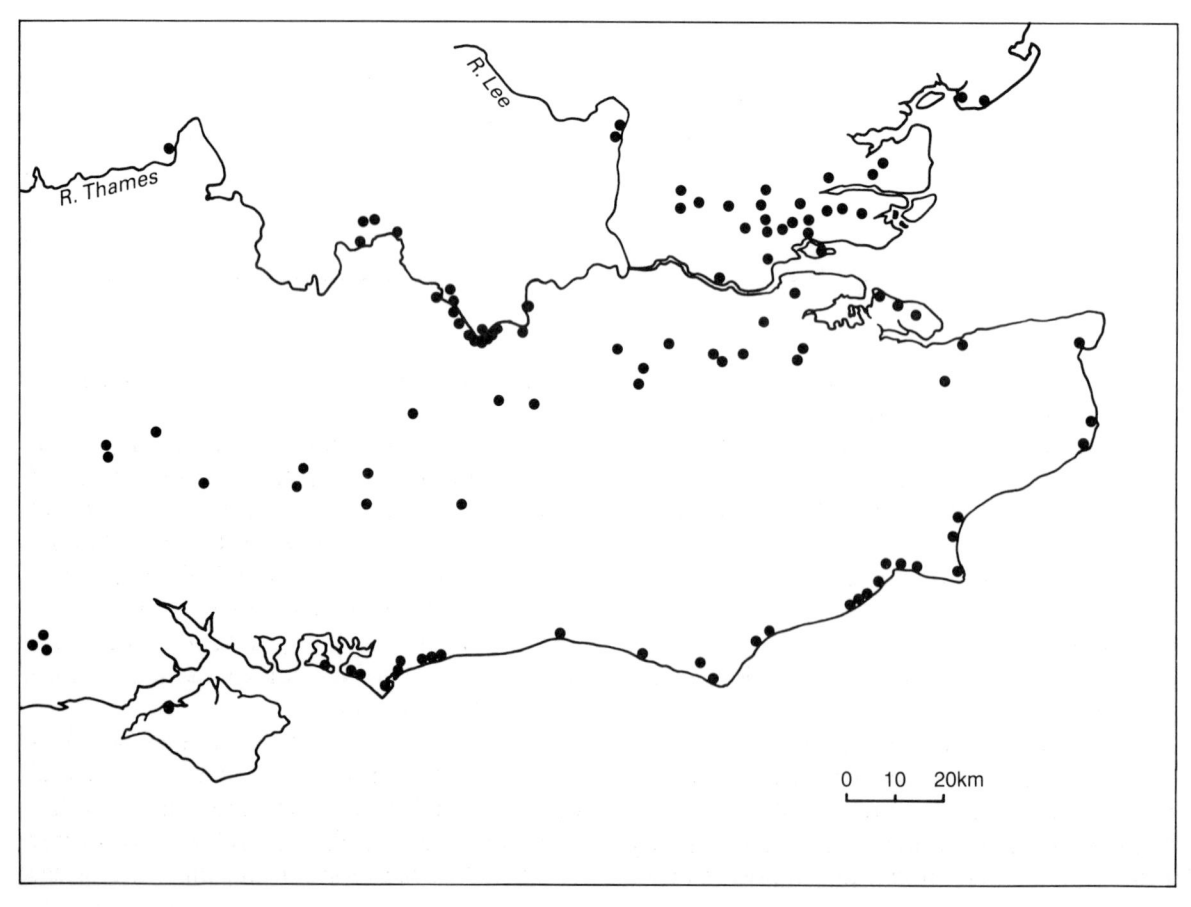

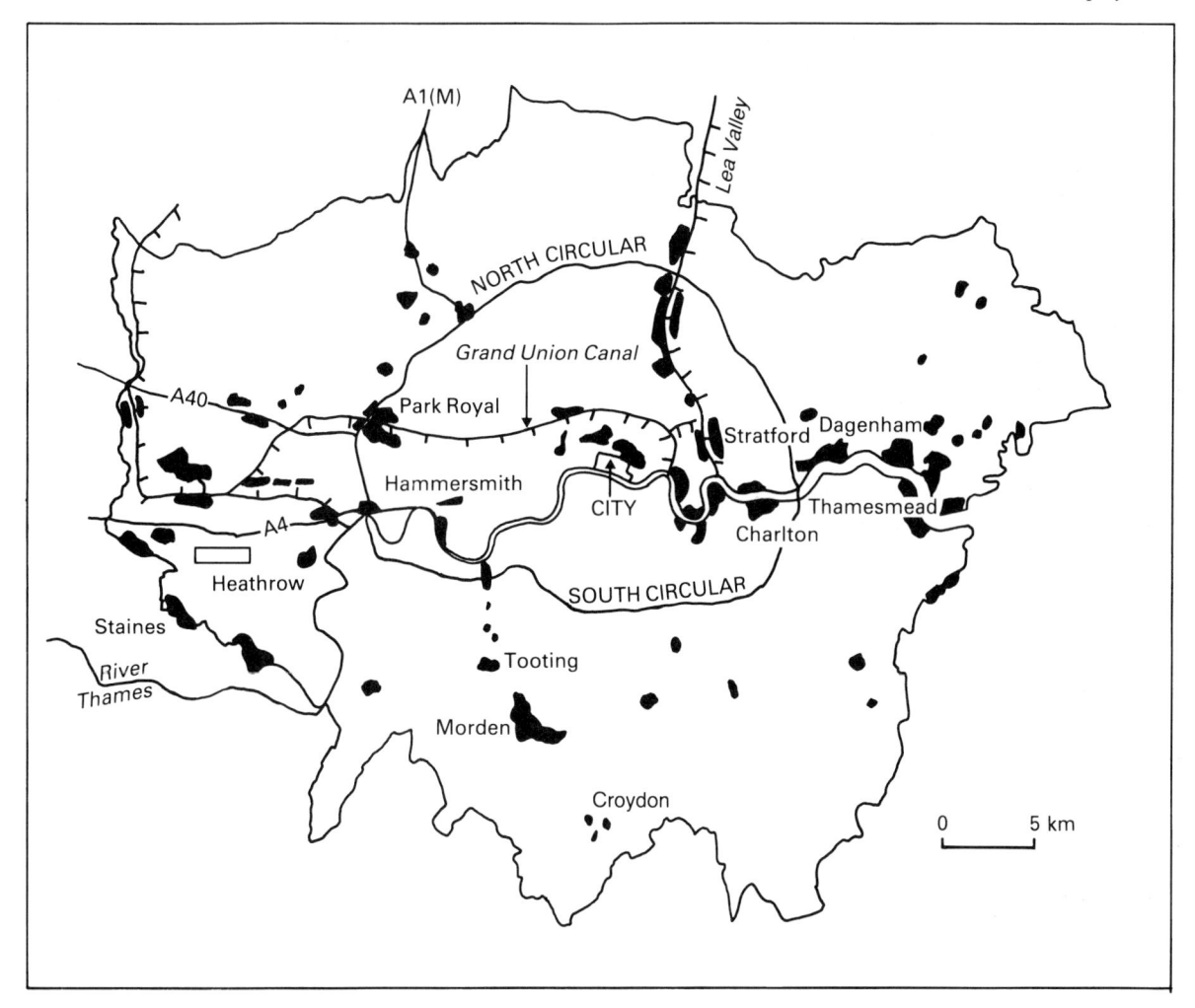

Figure 3.15 Major industrial areas in London

the Thames are large power stations, gas works and the huge Ford car factory at Dagenham. On the edge of the estuary, where the water is deep and the land flat, are the large oil refineries. Those at Canvey Island and the Isle of Grain were developed in the early 1960s, the former dangerously close to a densely-populated holiday resort.

Inner London away from the river has a number of specialised industrial districts. In the seventeenth century, Huguenot immigrants from France started making textiles in Spitalfields. This industry was continued by Jews from Eastern Europe in the early twentieth century and, since 1955 by Asians. Shoreditch has long been a furniture-making area, and Hatton Garden continues its tradition of jewellery manufacture.

These inner-city industries are mainly small scale. Many are family firms operating out of converted houses. The factories are often old and on several storeys, while the manufacture itself is labour intensive and skilled. Many firms are tied to the area by the pool of local workers and by established linkages between one firm and another. It is these linkages which produce the clustering of firms.

Nineteenth-century industries relied on transport by river and rail. Inner-city areas were well connected and close to the main markets within London. After the First World War, transport by lorry became more important. Inner areas suffered, as they still do, from narrow streets and congestion of traffic. Increasingly, industry sought locations in outer areas of London along main roads. **Ribbons** of factories developed along the A4, A40 and other roads leading out of the city. Inter-war **industrial estates** were part of this change, the largest being at Slough and Park Royal. Such estates had the advantage of keeping industry separate from housing. Individual firms on the estate gained from the proximity of other, linked firms. Services were provided, such as power stations, reservoirs, industrial clinics and training centres.

Park Royal (Figure 3.15) was built on the site of the Royal Agricultural Society show ground in north-west London. The site had been developed during the First World War for munitions factories and as a horse compound for the Royal Army Service Corps. The empty factories provided a base for the first firms which moved on to the site in 1925. These factories reflected the growing needs of people in the inter-war period, making cars, kitchen equipment, radios and cosmetics. They were some of the first to use mass-production techniques, and the main source of power was electricity: Park Royal was a manifestation of an emerging consumer society.

Manufacturing industry in London has declined since 1945, and especially since 1973. This has been largely because of foreign competition and a world-wide trade recession affecting industry everywhere. Mechanisation and improved technology has inevitably produced serious job losses in some sectors. In addition, many multi-national corporations have moved their plants to cheap-labour locations overseas.

The effects of the closure or contraction of some firms has been compounded by the decentralisation of others. London suffers from several disadvantages by comparison with areas beyond the Green Belt. Land and labour are more expensive, and factories are often old fashioned and with less room to expand. The environment is less attractive, road access poor, and the workforce may lack the skills needed for the growing high-tech industry.

Until recent years, decentralisation was encouraged by government policy. After 1934, governments offered special incentives to encourage industries to move out of London into areas with higher unemployment: the **assisted areas**. From 1947, a permit, the **Industrial Development Certificate (IDC)**, has been required for new factory building over a certain size. The new towns and expanded towns also attracted many firms out of the capital.

The decline of London's manufacturing base has inevitably led to unemployment in other sectors of the economy which served the factories: transport, distribution and construction (Table 3.5). By 1985, one in seven of all jobs which had existed ten years previously had gone.

Table 3.5 Numbers employed in manufacturing industry and related activities, London, 1973 and 1983

	No. employed 1973	1983	% change
All manufacturing	924,000	594,000	−36
Metal manufacturing	20,000	10,000	−50
Engineering	405,000	266,000	−34
Distributive trades	529,000	459,000	−19
Transport, communication	420,000	340,000	−19
Gas, electricity, water	56,000	41,000	−27
Construction	197,000	144,000	−27

With the collapse of industries and dockland, large areas of land in London are derelict: they cannot be used without further treatment. Acts of Parliament in 1980 and 1982 made provision for local authority surveys of such land and made available reclamation grants for both private and public sectors. Local authorities can now be forced to auction off underused or unused vacant land. In 1981 an aerial survey showed that there were 4775 hectares of unused land in the GLC area.

In recent years, efforts have been made to regenerate industry in London. The Urban Programme of aid to local authorities has been used to provide small workshops, such as the 12 opened in Nathan Way, Greenwich in 1984. The Greater London Enterprise Board (GLEB) invested £32 million in 179 projects in 1984. But it is in dockland that the most important initiatives have been taken.

Dockland

By 1799 the river-borne trade of London had grown to such an extent that space for further ships to load and unload was limited. In that year a Royal Commission recommended that dock basins should be built as a solution to the river's problems. The first to be opened were the West India Docks on the Isle of Dogs in 1802. The remaining dock basins were built throughout the nineteenth century, the last being at Tilbury. They are all to be found in the deeper waters downstream from the last bridge over the Thames, Tower Bridge (see Figure 3.16).

As the dock basins were carved out of the land, the waste material was deposited on marshy land around the East End. Basins were cut off from the river by lock gates. The area of waterfront was thus increased, and water levels could be controlled. The basins were enclosed by high walls for security against thieves. Around the docks were warehouses, railway sidings and related industries, such as furniture manufacture and food processing. Some homes were built for wealthier shipowners, but most of the Victorian housing developments in the East End were high density and low quality.

The docks began to decline after the Second World War. During the war itself a third of all warehouses were lost to bomb damage, and 50% of the population evacuated. But the real problem was simply a decline in volume of trade handled by the older docks. Many of these were too small, or the water too shallow, for modern ships. They suffered competition from the east coast ports, notably Felixstowe, and from Tilbury itself which had roll-on/roll-off facilities and a container terminal. The use of containers and new bulk-handling methods greatly reduced the volume of labour needed to run the docks. The number of registered dock workers in London fell from 25,500 in 1965 to 4130 in 1981. With the spin-off effect on other related industries it was estimated that 150,000 jobs of all types were lost between 1965 and 1978 as a result of dock closures. The tonnage of trade

Figure 3.16 London docks, with dates docks opened. All except Tilbury have now closed.

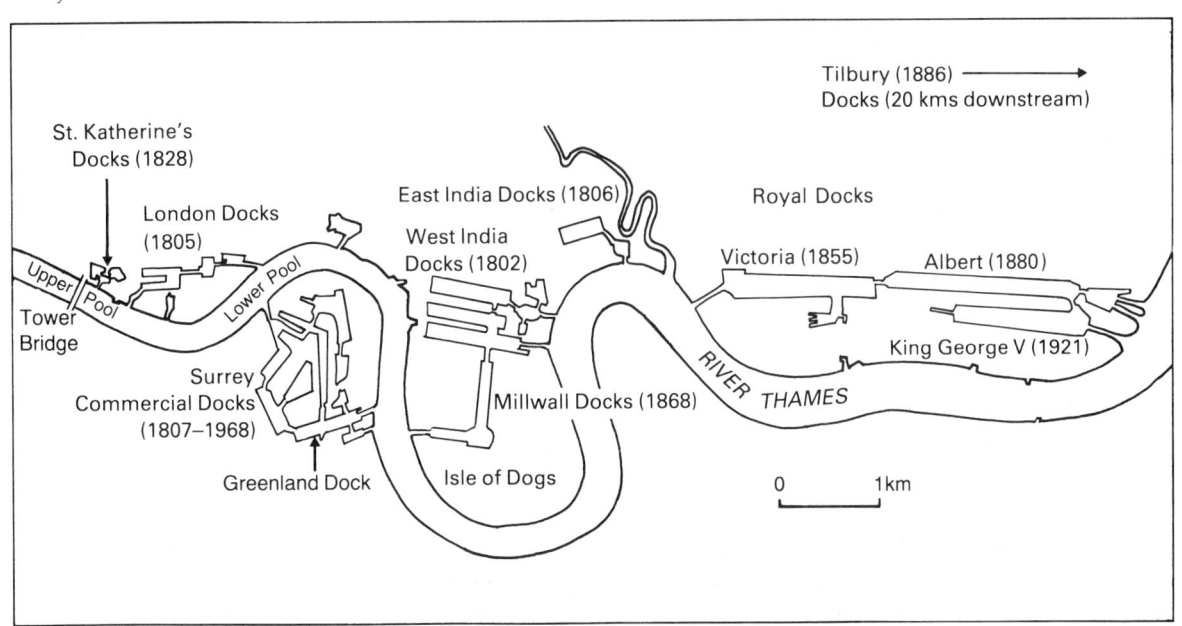

handled by the London docks fell from 56 million tonnes in 1970 to 39 million in 1981. All the docks except the Tilbury Docks have now closed, from the London and St Katherine's Docks in 1968 to the Royal Docks in 1981.

During the period 1968 to 1981 the docks were controlled by the Port of London Authority, the GLC and the borough councils. A **Docklands Joint Committee** was formed in 1974 and its plan, published in 1976, included proposals to double the population living in the area, attract new industry, build a tube line and construct a new river crossing. Partly because of lack of money, little happened before these schemes were scrapped by an incoming Conservative administration in 1979. Other schemes suggested for the Isle of Dogs in this period included an international exhibition centre, a huge park, a Disneyland-style development, a Channel Tunnel rail terminal, a holiday village complex and an international heliport.

An important question was whether or not to fill in the docks. The London Docks and Surrey Docks were filled, but not those in the Isle of Dogs and elsewhere. This was partly because of expense. Using arisings (excavated material from building sites), infilling cost £400,000 per hectare in 1981. Using marine dredged aggregate, it cost £750,000 per hectare. Another consideration was the amount of compensation that would have to be paid to the small number of remaining industries still importing materials by water, such as the timber and flour mills on the Isle of Dogs. Eventually, it was appreciated that the dock basins could be made into attractive waterfront locations for new buildings, and that they could be used for recreational purposes.

In 1981 the government set up the **London Docklands Development Corporation** to replace the Docklands Joint Committee. The LDDC was based on the successful new towns' Development Corporations, and comprised a body of experts who, while appointed by the government, were semi-autonomous in operation. It was the product of a Tory administration and, in line with government policy, aimed to attract private investors into the area. The LDDC was given three powers:

(i) To buy land from the main landowners (the local authorities, the Central Electricity Generating Board and others).
(ii) To produce land use plans for the area.
(ii) To build new roads, lay sewers, drains and power cables, construct factories and provide an environment which would be attractive to private developers.

The underlying principle is that of **demand-led planning**. The LDDC sets out the broad outlines of which type of activities should go where, but a great deal depends on the private investors' wishes. In other words, plans for the area are as much a response to demand for the land as a preconceived view of the needs of the area.

In its own terms the LDDC has been outstandingly successful, attracting a wide range of firms and transforming the environment of dockland. Between 1981 and 1985 it spent £230 m, but at the same time claimed to have attracted over £1000 m of private investment into the area. Above all, the LDDC has successfully changed the image of dockland from that of a run-down, depressed inner-city area to that of a fast-moving region with potential. Land which was previously idle has been put into use and the rise in land values to over £1 m per acre reflects this achievement.

Between 1981 and 1987 as many as 8000 jobs were created in dockland, and in 1984 job gains exceeded losses for the first time in decades. But few of these were the full-time jobs in manufacturing industry that the local people needed, most being in printing, publishing, leisure, retailing and personal services. In the next few years a high proportion will be in banking and finance. Given levels of investment in the area (as high as £1500 million, 1981–87), this works out at an expensive £180,000 per job created. Many of these jobs have simply moved from other parts of London. Meanwhile, the closure of existing firms in dockland has continued, so that overall employment in the area has risen only slightly.

The LDDC has been bitterly opposed by local residents and the borough councils. A **Joint Docklands Action Group** was formed to oppose what to many seemed a case of big money pushing the people out. The LDDC was a product of Conservative government policy in an area which has traditionally shown Labour Party support. Where the Corporation felt it was being decisive, others saw it as autocratic. Certainly, the powers of the LDDC have enabled it to proceed against the wishes of local people and councillors. It has encouraged the development of expensive houses which local people cannot afford, and jobs which do not match their skills. Where private enterprises have built offices, local people would like to have seen good-quality council houses. In some areas, access to the river and riverside walks has been lost to development schemes. In 1986, Rupert Murdoch's News International shifted printing of *The Times* and *The Sun* from Fleet Street to a new, automated works in Wapping, causing

Figure 3.17 Changes in the location of major national newspapers

A Former location (A) Present location *new newspapers
A News International *(Times, Sunday Times, Sun, News of the World)*: moved 1986
B Associated Newspapers, Printers *(Daily Mail, Mail on Sunday, London Evening Standard)*: moved 1988
C *Daily Telegraph, Sunday Telegraph*: moved 1987
D *Guardian*: moved 1987
E *Observer*: moved 1988
F *Financial Times*: moved 1988
G Fleet Holdings *(Daily Express, Sunday Express, Daily Star)*
H Mirror Group *(Daily Mirror, Sunday Mirror, Sunday People)*
I *Today**
J *Independent**: published from City Road but printed outside London

WOULD YOU BUY A NEWSPAPER FROM THIS MAN?

☐ Murdoch made £47,000,000 profit last year from his British Newspapers (**£900,000 a week**). BUT that was not enough to finance his American empire building plans.

☐ So he **sacked** 6,000 secretaries, cleaners, drivers, engineers, printers, journalists, clerical, computer, sales and warehouse staff.

☐ He was advised by his solicitors to cause a strike as this was 'the cheapest way to dispense with the workforce,'. He made no redundancy payments and will pay no pensions. If Murdoch succeeds, your employer may try it.

☐ Murdoch needs you to buy his papers to run '**Colditz Wapping**'.

DON'T LET HIM GET AWAY WITH IT!
PLEASE DON'T BUY

The Sun · The Times · News of the World · Sunday Times

Published by Southwark Trades Council. Printed by Southwark TU(SU) 12 Braganza Street, SE17

Figure 3.18 In 1986 Rupert Murdoch moved his printing presses from Fleet Street to dockland. The new automated print works required less labour. Redundant workers dubbed the closely guarded buildings 'Colditz Wapping'.

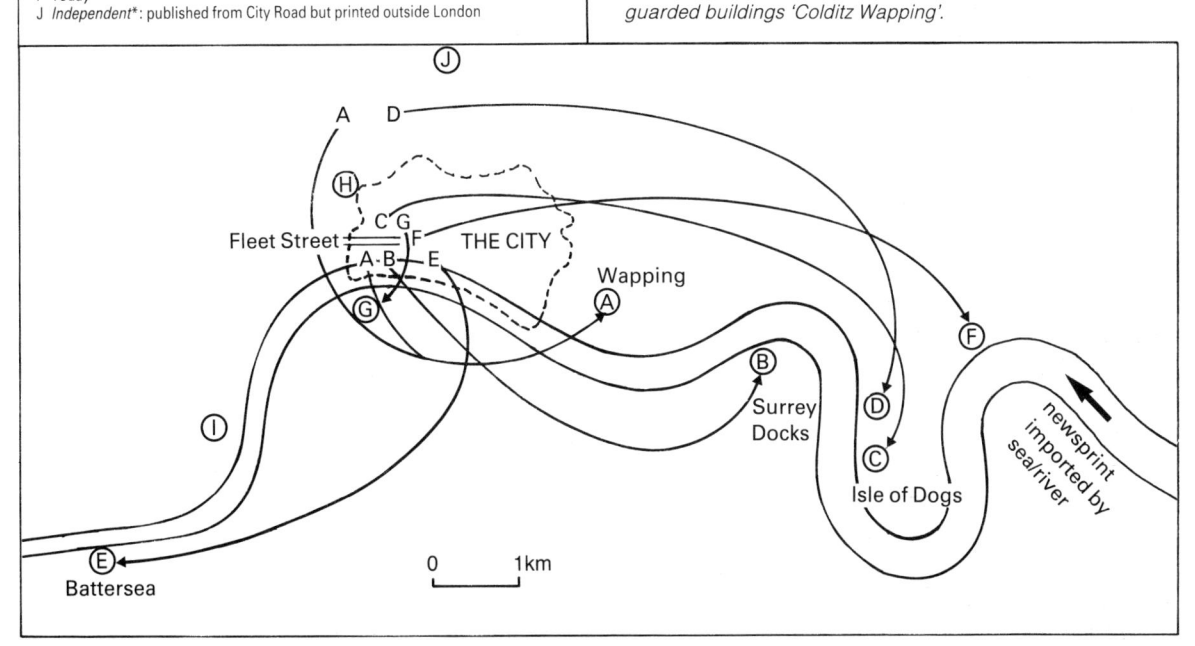

picketing disturbances and protests in the area. This was taken as further evidence that the LDDC could actually mean local people *losing* jobs rather than gaining them (Figures 3.17 and 3.18).

> **Study question**
>
> What were the arguments for and against relocating newspaper works from Fleet Street to dockland?

St Katherine's Dock

St Katherine's Dock closed in 1969. The closest dock to the heart of London, it had the greatest potential for development as a tourist and office centre. It was purchased from the Port of London Authority by the GLC, who converted the dock basins into moorings for private yachts and a historic ships marina. The World Trade Centre and a new hotel were built around the western dock, and warehouses were converted into shops, offices and pubs. Three hundred houses, for sale and rent from the local authority, were built on the southern edge.

> **Study question**
>
> Who do you think will be most powerful in determining the future of London's development over the next 30 years – the planners, the property developers, conservationists or local communities?

Despite the fact that, of five original warehouses, only one is now left, St Katherine's is generally regarded as a successful development. It is environmentally attractive and popular with visitors. The scheme did not, however, generate many jobs suitable for the former dock workers.

Surrey Docks

The Surrey Docks were the largest area of docks on the south bank of the river. Derelict since 1968, development of the site began in the 1970s. Many of the dock basins were filled in, and houses built for sale and rent. In 1983 the London Docklands Development Corporation took control of the area and produced further plans for housing, factory units, offices and a district shopping centre.

The history of the Greenland Dock in the Surrey Docks provides a good example of the conflict produced by the LDDC redevelopment schemes. In the 1970s, empty warehouses around the dock were occupied by small industries with a local labour force. In 1980 there were about 500 jobs in these firms. However, the LDDC wished to convert the dock into a marina surrounded by expensive houses and a number of offices: all 500 jobs were forcibly relocated, some to places as far away as Essex. The local people therefore lost a source of employment, and have gained little from new properties well beyond their purchasing power.

Isle of Dogs

The Isle of Dogs comprises the West India and Millwall Docks. Surrounded by a meander loop of the Thames, it has suffered from poor communications with the rest of London. Today, it is the heartland of LDDC redevelopment schemes. In 1980 much of the Isle was designated as one of eleven Enterprise Zones in the UK. The aim of the Zone was to create a free-trade atmosphere to stimulate private investment in the area. From 1980 to 1990, firms moving into the Zone are exempted from Development Land Tax and rates. Planning permission is easier to acquire, and the government has agreed to minimise the number of official returns that firms in the area will normally be required to submit.

The Enterprise Zone has attracted a large number of firms. Several film and TV companies have moved in, as well as the printing presses of the *Daily Telegraph* and *Guardian*. The 1.5-hectare Fred Olsson warehouses, built in 1969, are being converted into one of the largest sports centres in Europe. Canary Wharf, a 30-hectare site, could become a major financial area, with up to 12.2 million square feet of offices, hotels and shops (page 52).

However, the Enterprise Zone has been criticised on several grounds. It is felt that, rather

Employment

WHY MOVE TO THE MIDDLE OF NOWHERE, WHEN YOU CAN MOVE TO THE MIDDLE OF LONDON?

Main features of Enterprise Zones

Nature and purpose

The Government is setting up a number of Enterprise Zones (EZs). The idea is to see how far industrial and commercial activity can be encouraged by the removal of certain tax burdens, and by relaxing or speeding up the application of certain statutory or administrative controls. The Zones will last for 10 years and it is hoped that the first ones will come into effect this summer.

Eleven sites have been announced as prospective EZs. They vary widely, but all contain land ripe for development. In size they range from about 50 to over 400 hectares (about 125 to over 1000 acres). EZs are not part of regional policy, nor are they directly connected with other existing policies such as those for inner cities or derelict land. The sites chosen will continue to benefit from whatever aid is available under these policies.

Location and further information

The EZ sites are in Corby, Dudley, Hartlepool, the Isle of Dogs (in London's docklands), Newcastle/Gateshead, Salford/Trafford, Speke (Liverpool) and Wakefield in England; the lower Swansea Valley in Wales; Clydebank in Scotland; and Belfast, Northern Ireland.

At the end of this booklet is a list of addresses from which further information on the individual Enterprise Zones can be obtained.

Benefits

The following benefits are available, for a 10-year period from the date each Zone comes into effect, to both new and existing industrial and commercial enterprises in the Zones:

i. Exemption from Development Land Tax.
ii. Exemption from rates on industrial and commercial property.
iii. 100% allowances for Corporation and Income Tax purposes for capital expenditure on industrial and commercial buildings.
iv. Applications from firms in EZs for certain customs facilities will be processed as a matter of priority and certain criteria relaxed.
v. Industrial Development Certificates are not needed.
vi. Subject to the passage of the Employment and Training Bill, employers will be exempt from industrial training levies and from the requirement to supply information to Industrial Training Boards.
vii. A greatly simplified planning regime; developments that conform with the published scheme for each Zone will not require individual planning permission.
viii. Those controls remaining in force will be administered more speedily.
ix. Government requests for statistical information will be reduced.

Figure 3.19 Advertisement outlining the advantages of locating in the Enterprise Zone on the Isle of Dogs

than create new jobs, the Zone might simply attract firms from outside the area; jobs would merely be transferred in from elsewhere. Furthermore, firms outside the Zone might find it hard to compete with rivals inside the area. Areas in the near vicinity of the Zone might be particularly depressed: no new firm would ever choose to locate near an Enterprise Zone when

Figure 3.20 Recent developments in dockland

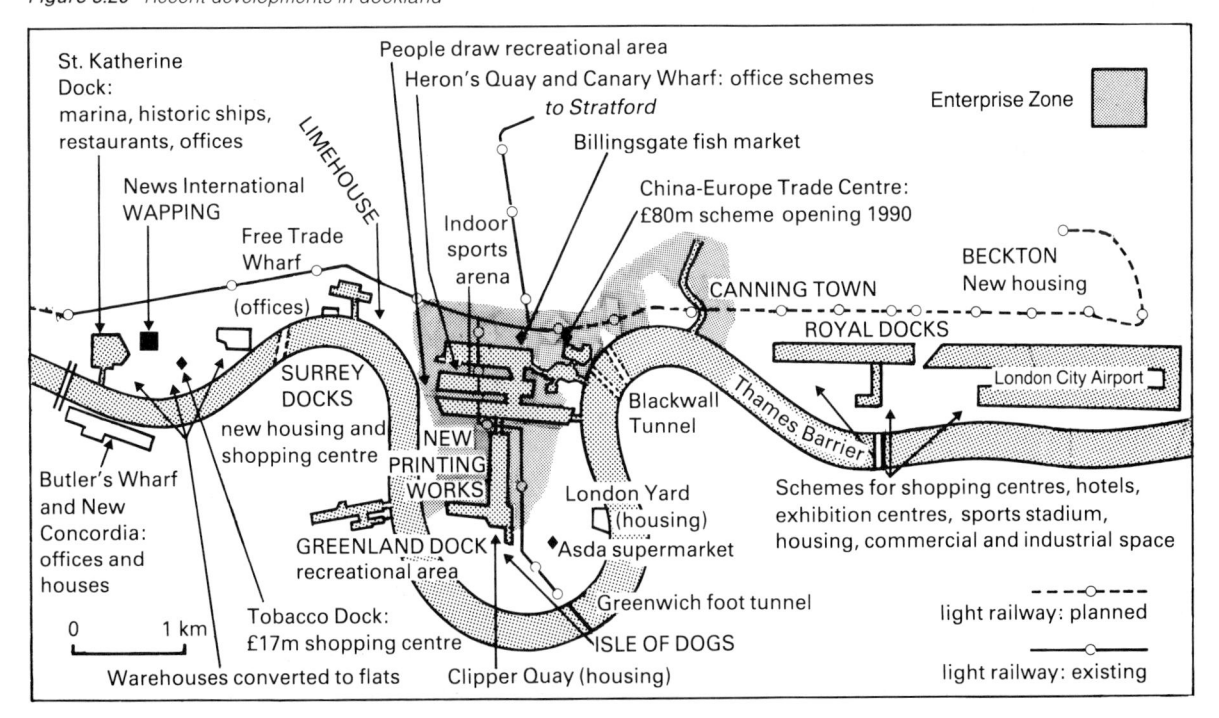

there are so many advantages to be gained from locating in it. Once again, the price of job creation in the Zone would be the loss of jobs elsewhere. Because activities in the Zone do not need planning permission, unsightly buildings might be created. The proposal to build three skyscrapers 850 feet high in Canary Wharf was strongly opposed by amenity groups who felt that they would dwarf historic views of the Royal Naval College from Greenwich Park.

In 1984, Asda opened a large supermarket on the eastern edge of the Isle of Dogs, costing £6 million. It was significant that the opening of the store was delayed for 18 months because narrow swing bridges over the entrances to docks were a problem for delivery lorries. The inaccessibility of the Isle of Dogs has been partially overcome with the construction of the light railway, linking the area to the City and Mile End (Figure 3.20).

Study activity

In the mid-1980s one of the main controversies in dockland was the proposal to build a £1.5-billion financial centre at Canary Wharf in the Isle of Dogs (Figure 3.20), including three office blocks each 850 feet high. Read these views of local people and summarise the main arguments for and against the scheme:

'Frankly, it's just a rich man's development.
'It will provide some jobs for people here but not that many. If there are jobs going then we should be given preference.'
Perry Olson, unemployed, Alpha Grove

Pupils at George Green School on the Island's southern tip were hopeful that Canary Wharf might improve their job prospects when they leave school.
Terriann Sullivan, age 15, said: 'I'm leaving school next year and I want to get an office job. It would be great if there was something for me at Canary Wharf, but I am not so sure there will be many jobs for me and my friends there.'
Her friend Kelly Marsh, also 15, said: 'It's a good idea if it does provide people here with jobs. I'm also leaving school next year and I would like to think I could get a job there.'

Dionne Church, aged 21, who has one child and lives in Stewart Street, said: 'Yes, it will bring some jobs, but I want to know how many will go to Islanders.
'There is a real need for more employment round here. Most of the companies that used to be here have gone. My husband, who is a warehouseman, has to work at Croydon and there are a lot of people like him.
'My other worry is that Canary Wharf might push up the price of houses round here. Already the cost of property has gone up enormously and it is very difficult for local people to try and buy a home of their own.'

'IT'S A BLOODY EYESORE!'

Chris Holland, who runs Holland's Stores in Castalia Square, hit out at the proposals.
'It's a bloody eyesore,' he stormed. 'I am against the whole concept. I don't like the accent on offices – offices don't produce anything but paper.'
The 59-year-old ex-docker added: 'I don't think it will do much for the jobs situation round here. What we need is industry.
'I also think that local people have not been given enough say. This is our Island and we should be able to have some say in what happens here.'

'I think it will do good for the area. I've been here three years and in that time I've seen things pick up enormously in that short time.
'I only used to have one or two bar staff. Now I've got six and a cleaner – and that's all because of what has been happening down on the Island. It must mean a lot of work for people on the Island.'
Bob Baverstock, publican, Brunswick Arms

Employment

'I don't like tower blocks and I think the traffic will become even worse if the scheme goes ahead. 'I hope Canary Wharf will mean definite jobs for people here.'
Tony Wisewell, youth worker, George Green School

'In the past when firms have moved here they have brought their own people with them and Islanders have not benefitted very much.'
'Canary Wharf must provide jobs for people living here.'
Dawn Ford, mother, Stewart Street

Royal Docks
The Royal Docks closed in 1981, leaving 96 hectares of water and 180 hectares of land idle. The focus for regeneration of the area has been the STOLPORT (London City Aiport) described on page 62. In 1987, three further schemes were being considered which, if carried out, would be even more dramatic than the developments on the Isle of Dogs. Worth about £1700 million between them, the plans include 4500 houses, 2 million square footage of retailing space, an equally large area of offices, provision for hi-tech industry, hotels, an exhibition centre and a large sports stadium. Construction of the light railway into the area, if completed, would no doubt further increase economic potential.

It is instructive to compare these schemes with the proposals of the local borough councils and the GLC, published as 'The People's Plan' in 1983. This plan aimed to use the land to deal directly with the perceived needs of local residents. It envisaged retaining some of the docks for cargo handling, as well as constructing a new container terminal. Ship repair and restoration would be revived and industry encouraged by the construction of new factory units, some of which would be run by local co-operatives. Public housing with gardens would be built, along with child-care facilities, local shops and parks. The airport would not be permitted, and office developments would also be discouraged.

Revision

1 Why was there an office building boom in London in the mid-1980s?
2 Why do specialised office districts form in central London?
3 What are the most important trends in retailing in London at present?
4 Why has manufacturing industry declined in London over the last 20 years?
5 What attempts are being made to regenerate dockland in London?

4

Transport

In every large city, traffic congestion and the financing of public transport are important issues. The problems involved tend, however, to be most intractable in cities so old that they were already largely built before the arrival of cars. London is one such place.

In recent years, successive administrations have tried to reduce the level of traffic on the streets of London by encouraging greater use of public transport. The central problem here is one of cost. Sufficient staff and rolling stock are needed to handle the volume of traffic during rush hours, but these same staff and equipment need to be paid for and maintained at other times of the day, when relatively idle. In the year 1983–4 the GLC subsidised public transport to the tune of £32.4 per person living in London.

Between 1966 and 1980 the number of people commuting into central London fell by over 13%, from 1.2 million to 1.05 million. The proportion using private transport rose slightly during this time, but was always less than 20% of all commuters.

> **Study activity**
>
> Conduct a survey to discover why some people drive to work while others use public transport. What distinguishes these two groups? Do the results of your survey suggest anything that could be done to encourage more people to use public transport.?

Railways

London is a product of the railway era. It had reached its present population size by 1900, before the first cars were seen on the streets. Because Britain was one of the first countries to experience the Industrial Revolution, London grew to a great size before other world cities, growing fastest during the period of railway expansion from 1860 to 1900.

The first line in London was built between Greenwich and Southwark in 1836. By 1900 the railway companies had purchased 160 hectares of central London, 5.4% of the total area. At least 120,000 poor people were uprooted in the process of rail development, because it was economical to demolish low-quality housing to make room for the lines. Figure 4.1 shows the routes taken by the lines constructed in the late Victorian era.

There were other reasons why a disproportionately large number of working-class housing areas were chosen as routes by the railways. Because most of the residents were tenants, it was easy for landlords to evict them. Furthermore, many people were only too pleased to see the slums being demolished. Factories were rarely knocked down to make way for railways. The railway companies preferred to pass through a small number of large estates rather than negotiate with many landlords, each controlling a small plot. Most industrial concerns were built on such small plots, purchased for a specific factory, while the larger estates were mainly residential. It was houses, therefore, which were swept away to make room for the railways.

Zones of blight were created along the new railway lines. Many displaced people moved only short distances, renting properties near their former homes. This created overcrowded conditions in these reception areas. Railway

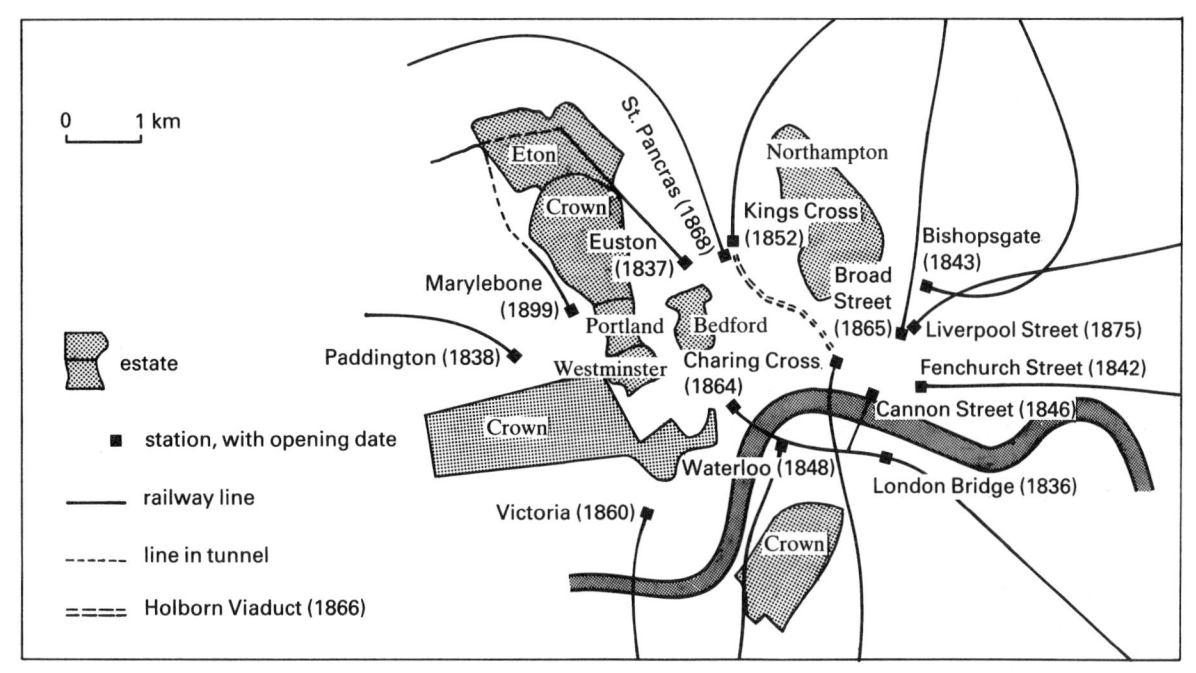

Figure 4.1 The main railway lines and stations built in Victorian London. Railways were blocked by some landowners, such as the Crown or Duke of Bedford. Others required the line to pass under their land (Eton College). On the northern side of the river, expensive properties blocked lines from running down to the river.

lines restricted access to areas on either side of them, and houses along the lines were not improved as much as houses elsewhere. The railway arches, built to prevent street closures, attracted squatters and the homeless.

Railways encouraged the spread of suburbs, especially in the north east (Edmonton and Walthamstow). After 1861, railway companies were compelled to provide cheap workmen's tickets and lay on a special workmen's train each morning and evening. This encouraged the growth of lower-quality suburbs such as Battersea, Peckham and Lewisham. The employment created by railway development itself attracted people to London. By 1891 the number of drivers, guards, porters, clerks, and those running transport to the London stations numbered 260,000.

Railways are still vitally important in London. Electrification has reduced travel times and, despite the loss of some lines and several stations, in the mid-1980s nearly 400,000 commuters arrived in the central area by British Rail every morning rush hour. In 1986, work began on a new rail line which will run under the Thames through a disused tunnel at Blackfriars. The £54-million scheme will enable commuters to cross London by British Rail, with an uninterrupted link between Gatwick and Luton airports.

The most important recent railway development has been the construction of the Docklands Light Railway, the first new overground railway in London for over 50 years (Figures 3.20 and 4.2). The line has been built to improve the accessibility of dockland and to make it more attractive to potential private investors. One line runs east–west from Tower Hill, along disused rail lines and viaducts, then south through the Isle of Dogs to the old North Woolwich station. A second line runs north-south from the docks to Mile End. Demolition has not been necessary, because both lines follow existing rights of way. The first phase of the railway,

London

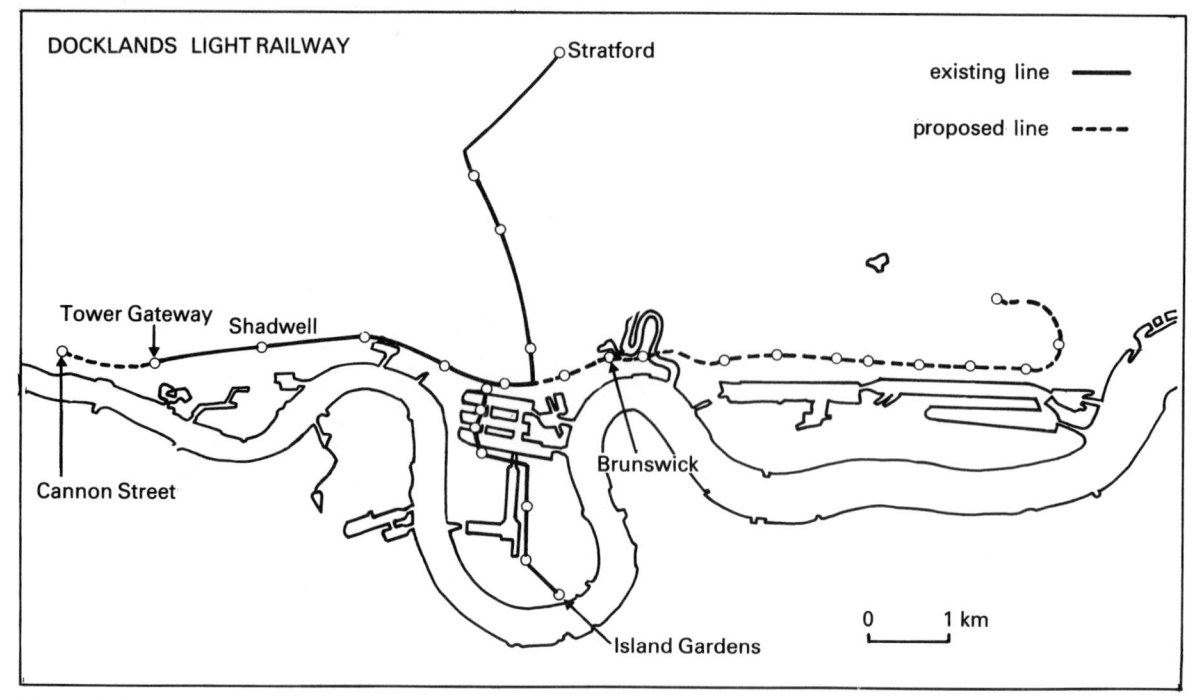

Figure 4.2 Docklands Light Railway – completed and proposed sections

costing £77 million, opened in 1987. Two extensions are now planned, one underground into the City, a second to the Royal Docks. If completed, these extensions will link the City directly with the dockland's airport.

London Regional Transport

The problem of expensive property demolition in the Victorian era was relieved by the construction of **underground railway lines**, the idea being that these new lines would encourage the middle classes to move further out of the centre. The first to be built was the Metropolitan Line from Paddington to Farringdon Street, begun in 1860. (Figure 4.3). The line was a success, carrying over 11 million passengers in the first year, and this encouraged other private developers to build lines. These included the District and Circle Lines after 1865, and the Central and Northern Lines at the turn of the century. In more recent years, further lines have been built to reduce street congestion: the Victoria Line between 1962 and 1971, and the Jubilee Line from 1970 to 1979. With the exception of the Waterloo and City Line, the whole network (400 km of track) is run by London Regional Transport. In the mid-1980s over 700 million passengers were carried each year, 3 million on an ordinary weekday. This number is still growing, putting pressure on both trains and stations.

In the morning rush hour, over half a million passengers use London Regional Transport's bus and underground services to reach a central destination. While buses are normally used for short distance journeys and railways for longer distances, the underground is used mainly for middle-distance journeys within London.

Buses have existed in London since the end of the nineteenth century. Horse-drawn omnibuses existed before the railway boom, and electric tramways were built to fill the gaps between railway lines. Since 1950, however, the bus service has declined. Because of traffic congestion, average speeds have fallen and the reliability of buses deteriorated. Low wages and unsocial hours have combined to create a shortage of both drivers and conductors.

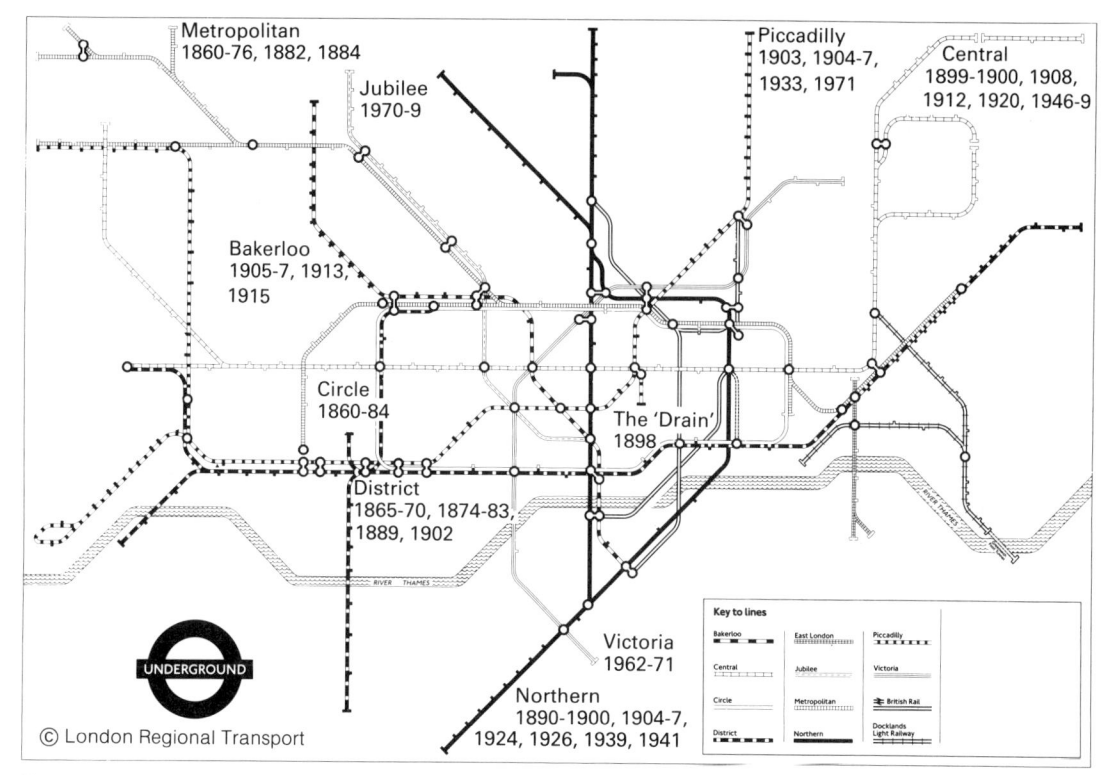

Figure 4.3 London's Underground network. The principle dates of construction of each line are shown in bold.

Since 1982 efforts to improve the system have been successful. The introduction of simplified and reduced fare systems, with Travelcards permitting travel on both bus and Underground, produced a 16% increase in passenger mileage on London Transport in 1983–4. This reduced the number of cars entering central London in peak hours by some 10%. A bus-lane programme has also increased speeds and service reliability.

Waterways

Before the coming of the railway, much trade in London was carried out using rivers and canals. Today, little of this type of trading remains. The number of passengers carried on the Thames has fallen from 20 million in 1870 to 3.5 million in 1985. Cargo handled by the Port of London fell from 53.2 million tonnes in 1971 to 35.3 million in 1981.

Although the volume of traffic is much reduced, two of London's canals, the Grand Union system and Lea navigation, are still maintained by the British Waterways Board for commerical cargo. The third, Regents Park Canal, is used for recreation only.

In 1985 the Thames Water Authority announced a £40-million plan to sponsor fast river buses. They hope to renovate old piers and build new ones with shops and restaurants attached. One such pier would serve the dockland's airport.

Roads

Traffic congestion in London is not a new problem. Descriptions of the city in the eighteenth century paint a picture reminiscent of conditions in poorer Third World cities today: a crush of carriages, with people and livestock battling over narrow, unsurfaced roads.

The development of the railway and underground network temporarily relieved the problem, but conditions worsened again around 1950. Many jobs remained concentrated in the central area (1.2 million in 1985). Lorries and coaches increased in size and number. The absence of a ring-road produced unnecessary through traffic. Much of central London was built before cars were seen on the streets, and could not be adapted without a massive programme of building demolition. In the 1950s and 1960s motorways were built from other parts of Britain to London, but they did not penetrate beyond the inner suburbs of the capital. The heavy traffic they generated disgorged on to the city's inadequate roads. The number of registered vehicles per kilometre of road (195) is almost twice that of other big cities in Britain.

Traffic congestion was not the only problem created by motor vehicles. People living on busy roads suffered increasing levels of noise and pollution from lead and carbon monoxide. On-street parking and large car parks spoilt the appearance of many areas. Each year from 1960 to 1980 between 700 and 900 people were killed on the roads of London.

A fundamental issue facing transport planners in all major cities is whether or not to improve provision for road traffic. Short-term improvements in road conditions may merely encourage more people to use cars rather than public transport. The increasing volume of road traffic then recreates the problems the planners were trying to solve, and on a larger scale.

Before the early 1960s, little money was invested in London's roads. Between 1919 and 1957 the limited finance available was spent on housing. After 1957, priority was given to building inter-city motorways. By 1960, congestion in London was becoming serious, and the Ministry of Transport commissioned two inquiries into the problem.

Colin Buchanan's report, **Traffic in Towns**, was published in 1963. The report suggested that it was possible to define an acceptable environmental standard in terms of noise, pollution and inconvenience, for any road. It was up to planners to restrict the volume of traffice in every road to a level which did not upset this standard. Buchanan also showed how the demolition of large numbers of buildings was going to be necessary to improve traffic flows in some cities.

A second report, published in 1961, was the **London Traffic Survey**. The results of this survey were incorporated into the GLC's **Ringway Plan** in 1966, itself part of the 1969 Greater London Development Plan. The Ringway Plan envisaged the construction of four ring motorways in London: one 4–5 km from the centre, one on the edge of inner London, one in the outer suburbs and one beyond the built-up area. The scheme was to be accompanied by the widening of many existing roads feeding the motorways.

The Ringway Plan was never implemented. GLC elections in 1973 were fought on the issue and won by the Labour party, opponents of the scheme. There were a number of strong arguments against the Ringways, not least the price-tag – £1000–£2000 million. The homes of 100,000 Londoners would have been demolished. Because more people would have been encouraged to use cars, the viability of public transport would have been further reduced, an unwelcome development from the point of view of those not owning a car.

A short stretch of inner urban motorway was, in fact, built in north London during the early 1960s by the Ministry of Transport. The Westway attracted much criticism from local people, and provided a useful case history for opponents of the Ringway Plan. The new motorway generated an extra 90,000 car journeys per day with the result that both it, and the roads it was designed to relieve, became congested. Today, therefore, London has only 90 kilometres of urban motorway – the Westway, and two sections in the East End leading to the Blackwall Tunnel.

From 1973 to its abolition in 1986, the GLC maintained a policy of discouraging motorists and encouraging the use of public transport. A key strategy was to limit the amount of space available for parking. Parking meters were introduced in 1958, since which time parking in many streets has been prohibited or restricted to permit holders. The number of parking spaces provided in new property developments has been controlled. Some car parks were closed by the GLC, the prices charged by others increased. In 1983 wheel clamps were introduced to deter illicit parking.

Priority has been given to public transport, cyclists and pedestrians. The creation of bus

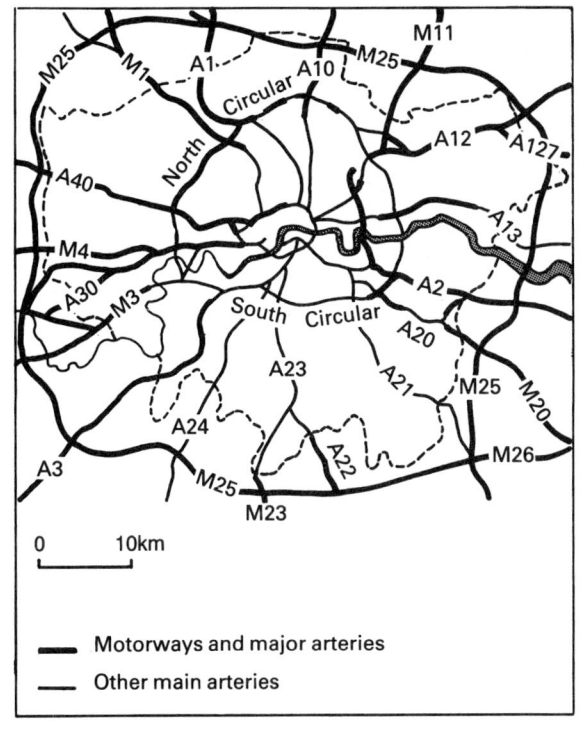

Figure 4.4 Major roads in London

lanes has reduced the road space available to cars at peak hours. Oxford Street was closed to private cars in 1972, paving the way for many similar developments. Over 400 kilometres of cycle routes were in use by 1986, with 73,000 Londoners cycling to work each day. In 1984, cheap taxi and dial-a-ride schemes for the disabled became a London-wide service. In 1985, parking on pavements in most streets became illegal. A night and weekend heavy-lorry ban was also implemented in 1986.

With the abolition of the GLC in 1986, control of major roads in London passed to the Department of Transport. The revelation that they had commissioned five studies into the possibility of major new road schemes within London reopened the question of inner-urban motorways for the first time since 1973. Several new roads were considered, including a widening of the South Circular, the construction of a new route from Shepherd's Bush to Battersea, and a major road in East London to connect with a new bridge over the Thames at Thamesmead.

The most important transport initiative in the 1980s was the completion of a ring-road around London, the M25. The road, which is 190 kilometres long and cost £1000 million, enables traffic from the Midlands and North to reach Channel ports without having to pass through London. It is equally important for local users starting and finishing journeys within five miles of the motorway. The new road takes the strain off the busy streets of London. Traffic on the North Circular is expected to fall by 7–13%. In London as a whole, traffic should be reduced by 3–5% of total movements, this figure being higher for heavy lorries. Hundreds of settlements around the ringway have also lost traffic which previously clogged their streets. The daily traffic flow in the small town of Westerham in Kent fell from 50,000 to 20,000 vehicles. Not only did life become quieter, people were happier to shop in the town and property prices rose.

The motorway is not, however, without its critics. By improving conditions for motorists, it may generate increased traffic on feeder roads: a level of 66,000 vehicles per day on the M1 in 1981 is expected to rise to 100,000 by 1996. Much Green Belt land has been lost to the road. It may act as a magnet to further commercial and industrial developments and, if this happens to too great a degree, it will accelerate the decline of inner London (page 18).

Most serious of all, however, has been the level of congestion on the M25 itself (Figure 4.5). The motorway has clearly generated a large volume of unexpected *new* traffic in addition to that which has been diverted on to it from existing roads. The original Department of Transport traffic forecasts have been shown to be underestimates, and too few lanes were built as a result of those figures. Congestion is worst in the

Figure 4.5 Traffic chaos on the newly-opened M25 in 1986

south-western sector around Staines and in the Dartford tunnels under the Thames. The number of vehicles passing through the Dartford tunnels doubled between 1980 and 1986 to 22 million a year, and this is expected to rise to 27 million by 1990. In 1986 a competition was held to design a new private enterprise crossing at Dartford, costing £100 million-plus, to relieve this bottleneck.

> **Study question**
>
> Why is it that roads in big cities always seem to be congested?

Airports

Heathrow began as a military airfield during the Second World War, and opened to civil traffic in 1946. It was ideally placed to assume the role of the capital's premier airport – close to the west side of London on the A4 (later M4), on flat, well-drained Thames gravels, and suitable meteorologically. It has one major limitation however: the population density in the surrounding area is quite high, and because of prevailing westerly winds the best approach paths are over the western suburbs of London. Furthermore, the growth of air traffic has tended to outstrip the ability of both the airport terminals and surface transport to cope. Heathrow handles more international passengers than any other airport in the world (30 million in 1985), it deals with 14% of the total value of the UK's world trade, and employs 60,000 people.

Gatwick airport began as early as 1930 but was not officially designated as London's second airport until 1953. Located 27 miles south of central London, it is well connected to the capital by road and rail. Expansion at Gatwick brought the number of passengers up to 14 million in 1984. Further growth is limited by the fact that the airport is close to built-up areas and is in an environmentally attractive area.

Between 1960 and 1984 there were five major reports analysing the proposals for a third airport to supplement Heathrow and Gatwick. Astonishingly, in view of the cost of these reports and the inquiries on which they were based, nothing was actually built as a result.

The most important of these inquires was the **Roskill Commission, 1968–71**. The Commission examined 78 possible sites and reduced this to a short-list of four: Thurleigh, Cublington, Nuthamstead and Maplin (Figure 4.6). These four were each subjected to cost-benefit analysis, which involved giving a financial cost figure to each of 20 variables affecting airport location. For each variable the figure given was the difference between the cost at that site and the cost at the cheapest of the four sites. On this basis, the Commission chose the site at Cublington, a village in rural Buckinghamshire well placed between London and Birmingham (Figure 4.6). One member of the Commission, Sir Colin Buchanan, disagreed with this decision because of the devastating effect such a new airport would have on the attractive environment of this unspoilt part of England. He was supported by a pressure group of local residents, environmentalists and the media. The outcry persuaded the government to reject the findings of the Commission and opt, instead, for the site at Maplin in Essex.

Figure 4.6 Existing and proposed airport sites around London

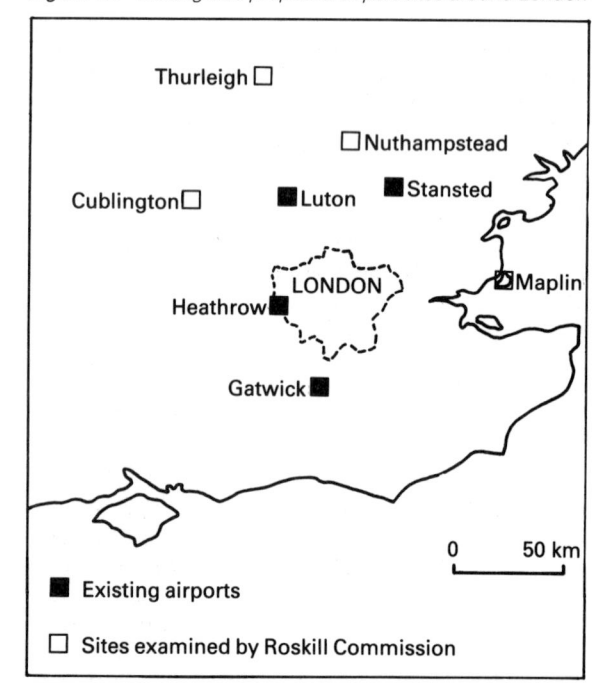

Maplin had certain advantages as a site: it was on the coast, and noise would disturb relatively few people. Inevitably, it had limitations. Being inaccessible, new surface routes would have had to be constructed into London. It would have been expensive to build the airport – some £650 million. The important wildlife of the area would have been disturbed, and an attractive stretch of coastline ruined. A new town to support the airport would also have covered 82 square miles of land.

Shortly after the government's decision had gone in favour of Maplin, three developments necessitated a rethink of the whole concept of the third airport. The 1973–4 oil price rises meant that air travel became more expensive, and the predicted volume of future air traffic demand was reduced. While the air traffic passing through London's airports rose by 12% each year from 1963 to 1972, the increase fell to under 3% over the years 1972 to 1976. Secondly, the increased size of aircraft meant that fewer aircraft were needed, and the number of air movements was reduced. Finally, the capacity of Heathrow and Gatwick was seen to be greater than had been forecast, because incoming traffic was becoming more evenly spread throughout the year. The noise problem at these sites was also being progressively reduced as new jets became quieter.

Throughout the post-war period, many authorities have favoured Stansted, a small airport 34 miles north east of London, as a possible major airport. The Eyre inquiry, which reported in 1984, proposed that Stansted should be expanded from a capacity of 350,000 passengers each year in 1984 to 15 million by 1990, rising to an eventual maximum of 25 million. Eyre considered that at anything above 25 million pas-

Table 4.1 Government forecasts of the impact of aircraft noise, 1976

		Population ('000) within the areas of three critical indices of aircraft noise and frequency (Noise and Number Index)		
		35 NNI (slight annoyance)	45 NNI (moderate annoyance)	55 NNI (high annoyance)
Heathrow	1972	2092	373	78
	1990	250	50	3.5
Gatwick	1972	30	2	1
	1990	2	1	0

Table 4.2 Main proposals of the 1984 Eyre Report on the site for a third London airport

Aim: Cater for an estimated increase of 40m passengers p.a. by 2000

Proposed expansion:

		Capacity million passengers p.a.	Build
Stansted	1984	0.35	
	1990	15	– fast rail link to London
	thereafter	25 maximum	– second terminal but not a second runway
Heathrow	1985	30	– a fifth terminal – direct British Rail link to London – improved road to London
	1996	53	

Table 4.3 Arguments for and against Stansted airport as a location for third London airport.

For Stansted	Against Stansted
1 Close to London Good surface transport	1 Loss of good agricultural land
2 An existing airport	2 Noise traffic nuisance and urban development would destroy character of the local area
3 Air traffic control would be satisfactory	
4 Flat terrain	3 Huge cost: £1 billion?
5 Only 17000 additional dwellings would be needed	4 Gives too much emphasis to the South East which is already economically dominant. Further depresses the status of areas outside the South East, to which people may wish to fly but cannot. The 'regional' share of total UK international traffic is rising.
6 Noise problem not great	
7 Boost to local economy	
8 80% of passengers using London's airports begin or end their journey in the South East	

sengers a year, the environmental impact of the expanded airport on the local area would become unacceptable. For this reason, much of the expected increase in air traffic would still have to be accommodated at Heathrow, and Eyre proposed that a fifth terminal should be added to the fourth opened in 1986. The passenger capacity would thereby rise from 28 million in 1984 to 54 million by 1995 (it had reached 39 million by 1987). Expansion of Heathrow, Gatwick and Stansted is now under way.

In 1987 the three London airports are to be joined by a surprising development on a site near the heart of London. The £18-million **London City Airport** is being built on a 360-hectare site in the Royal Docks, east of the City. It is sponsored by Brymon Airways, a subsidiary of De Havilland of Canada who make the 50-seater Dash–7 aircraft. This plane is the only type capable of using such a small runway: it is a short-take-off-and-landing aircraft (hence the name STOLport). The site is only six miles from the City, in terms of travel time considerably closer than Heathrow. With minimum delays between check-in and take-off, the airport expects to attract business travellers flying to Paris, Brussels, Frankfurt, Rotterdam, Amsterdam, Dublin and nine British cities. Brymon estimate that 490 people will be employed in the airport, with perhaps 5000 jobs generated in related industries developing around it. Local people and the GLC opposed the scheme, because of both the noise and potential danger of an airport in the middle of an urban area. The London Docklands Development Corporation commissioned a noise assessment report and, as a result of its findings, ensured that noise-protection measures were included in the airport design: a ban on helicopters and club or recreational flights; a limit of 30160 flights a year, or 120 a day on weekdays and 40 on Sundays and holidays; flight hours confined to 06.30–22.00 on weekdays and 09.00–22.00 on Sundays; a limit on aircraft types and length of runway; and the provision of noise barriers.

> **Study question**
>
> How do you think transport technology will develop in the next 20 years? What effect will this have on London?

> **Revision**
>
> 1 Describe and assess the measures that have been taken to deal with traffic congestion in London.
> 2 What factors have to be taken into account when determining the site of a new airport?
> 3 What transport developments are taking place in London's docklands? To what extent will these benefit or harm the interest of local people?

Table 4.4 Transport milestones

1800 –	First railway line (Greenwich to Southwark), 1836
	First Underground line (Metropolitan Line), 1860–63
	Cheap workmen's tickets, 1861
1950 –	Inter-city motorways, 1957–65
1960 –	Parking meters, 1958
	Buchanan Report, Traffic in Towns, 1963
1970 –	Victoria tube line, 1962–71
	Ringway (motorway box) Plan, 1966–73
	Jubilee tube line, 1970–79
1980 –	GLC abortive Fares Fair plan, 1984
	Wheel Clamp, 1984
	M25, 1983–87
	Eyre Report, 1984
	STOLPORT approved, open 1987
	Docklands Light Railway, 1985–87
	Thames Water Authority plan for new river buses, 1986
	East London River Crossing plan, 1986

5

London's physical environment

Water supply

Since 1974 London's water has been supplied by Thames Water, successor to the Metropolitan Water Board (established 1903). Thames Water is responsible for water supply, pollution control, flood alleviation, sewerage, navigation, fisheries and water-based recreation within the whole area drained by the River Thames and its tributaries. As with other water authorities in Britain, the breadth of its responsibilities is an example of **integrated river basin management** – a recognition of the fact that one aspect of a river basin (such as fishing) cannot be properly managed without consideration of other aspects (such as pollution). Thames Water can treat the river basin as a unit, transferring water from areas of surplus to areas of deficit, and organising the re-use of water down the length of the Thames.

With improving hygiene and the installation of central heating, washing machines and dishwashers, demand for water rises steadily by 1% per year. In the mid-1980s London used 440 million gallons of water per day, and since 1974 it has been the job of Thames Water to meet this demand. Eighty-five per cent of London's water comes from **reservoirs** filled by the Thames (Surbiton, Ashford Common, Hampton, Kempton Park, Walton-on-Thames) and the River Lea; with the exception of the Lea Valley reservoirs, these are connected to pipes carrying water eastwards under the city.

Use is also made of **groundwater aquifers** in the chalk and Lower Tertiary sands of the London Basin. As water is drawn out, the aquifer can be recharged with water from the Chilterns and North Downs. Water is pumped from the Berkshire Downs into the River Kennet near Newbury, from whence it flows into the Thames and is abstracted downstream. Much water is used more than once as it passes down the Thames. Forty per cent of London's water leaks out of the mains before it reaches consumers, and in 1983 Thames Water initiated a scheme to reduce this figure to 20%.

In the late 1980s a new £175-million ring main is being built around London (Figure 5.1). This will replace most existing mains pipes, many of which are over a hundred years old. The new ring will be gravity fed, saving pumping costs, and will be complete by 1994.

Thames Water is required under the 1974 Control of Pollution Act and EEC Directives to preserve the quality of river water. Monitoring devices check the river for pollution, and consent for discharging waste into the rivers can be given only by Thames Water. The Thames Bubbler, a floating oxygen-producing plant, is used to combat oxygen depletion after storms (when some sewage may be discharged into rivers) or after pollution incidents. The success of Thames Water was rewarded in 1985 when the company gained a contract from the Indian Government to clean up the Ganges.

Flooding

Floods can be caused by heavy rainfall, rapid snowmelt, inundation by high tides, or combinations of these. Straightening the river for navigation has reduced the length of channel able to hold the water. Before the growth of towns, water falling to the ground seeped slowly through soil and rock before reaching the river.

London

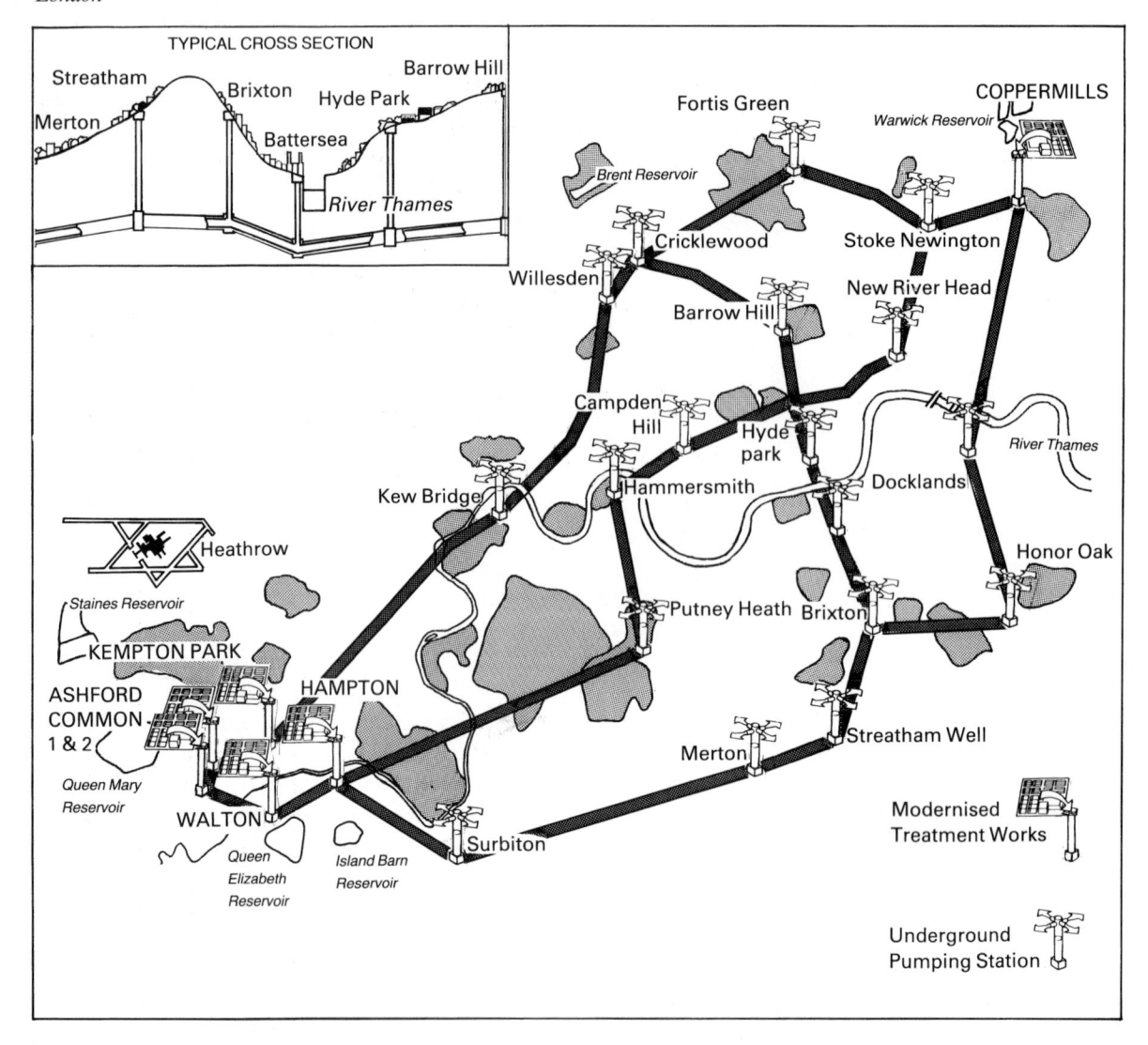

Figure 5.1. London's new ring main

Today, rain moves quickly from paved surfaces into sewers and the Thames. Both the volume of runoff and the speed with which it enters the river have increased. In the past, the Thames had areas such as the Hackney Marshes where the river could safely spill over. Gradually, such areas have been reclaimed and protected from flooding, increasing the danger elsewhere. A recent problem has been caused by a rising water table under London. Traditionally, the aquifer under the capital was pumped for water and, in the process, kept at a low level. Today, less is taken from this source and ground water levels are rising, increasing the danger of flood.

In the heart of London the greatest threat comes from a deep depression over the North Sea, forcing up the level of the Thames (Figure 5.2). Strong north-easterly winds can produce a tidal surge as high as 2 metres. The south-east of England is sinking at a rate of 30 centimetres per 100 years relative to sea level, a result of post-glacial readjustment, and this has also increased the likelihood of flood. Before its abolition, the GLC ran a public awareness campaign to alert Londoners to the danger (Figure 5.3).

London's physical environment

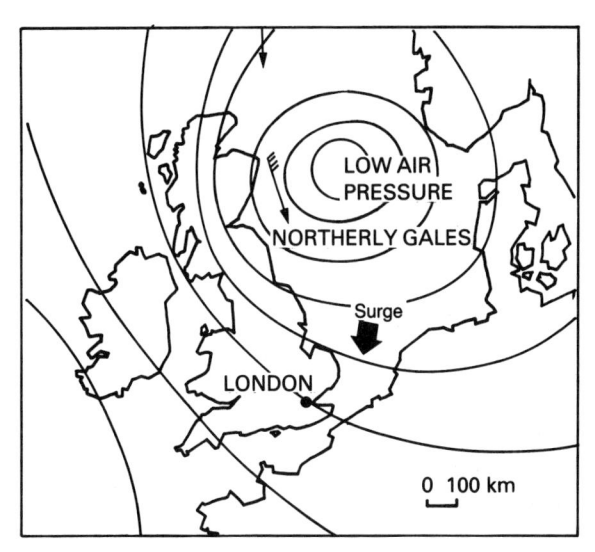

Figure 5.2 Synoptic conditions likely to produce high levels in the Thames

The Thames Water Board and local authorities have dealt with the flood hazard in several ways. Open spaces such as sports fields have been retained as spill-over areas and, where possible, the river channel has been enlarged. New building is restricted by local authority planners in areas of flood danger. Excess runoff can be diverted into reservoirs.

Figure 5.3 Warning to Londoners before the completion of the flood barrier

THAMES FLOODING

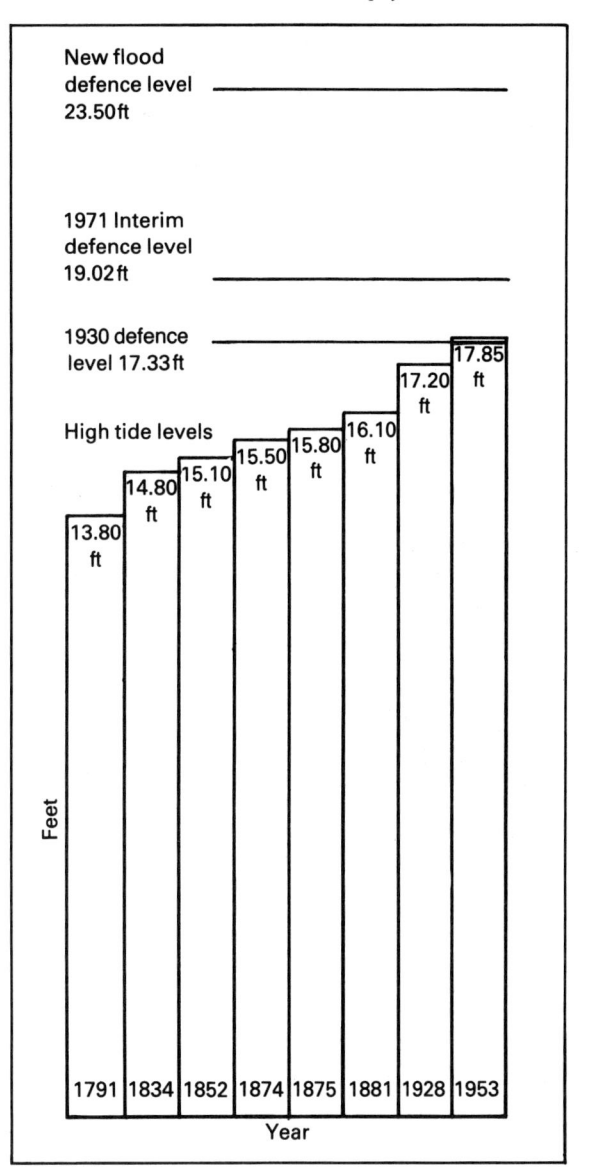

Don't wait until it happens.

If you live, work or travel in London you should learn your Thames flood drill **now**.

GLC
Working for London

Figure 5.4 High-tide levels and flood defence levels at London Bridge

In 1984 the GLC opened a £450-million **flood barrier** at Woolwich Reach. The barrier consists of ten movable steel gates pivoted on concrete piers, spanning the half kilometre across the Thames. The gates swing up to dam the river during a tidal surge, but allow traffic to pass at other times. The banks of the Thames have been raised below the barrier, down to Southend and the Isle of Grain. The London Weather Radar Scheme is also improving flood warnings within the capital area.

Figure 5.5 *The Thames flood barrier*

Sewers

Before 1859, inadequate sewage disposal was one of the greatest problems faced by the inhabitants of London. Many houses were connected to one of the 200,000 cesspits, themselves a health risk. Those without cesspits emptied chamber pots into the street. The flushing water closet came into use in the eighteenth century, but this merely worsened the problem for a city lacking sewers to carry the waste away. The few underground sewers which existed ran straight into the rivers, spreading cholera and turning the Thames into a foul drain. In 1858 a smell, known as the 'Great Stink', spread over London.

In 1855, the **Metropolitan Board of Works** was created to deal with the problem. It studied various schemes before appointing Joseph Bazalgette to carry out his plans for a new system. Over the next six years he built 20,000 kilometres of local sewers feeding into 700 kilometres of main sewers. These led the sewage by gravity down towards the Thames, but instead of flowing into the river, **intercepting sewers** took the waste out to the eastern edge of London. Here **treatment works** were built, north of the river at Barking and at Plumstead on the south bank. Storm relief sewers were also made to carry exceptional rain runoff directly into the Thames.

Between 1890 and 1913, two more intercepting sewers were laid north of the Thames, but Bazalgette's system is the basis of the modern network. In some British cities, such as Manchester, Victorian sewers have begun to collapse and in London Thames Water has embarked on a major repair and renovation scheme.

Air pollution

In many respects air pollution in London is less serious today than at any time for about two hundred years. The problem is still taken seriously, however, for although modern pollutants are less visible than those of the past, they are potentially as dangerous.

Burning coal was the main source of air pollution in London before 1960. Coal produces sulphur dioxide, nitrogen oxide and fine particles of soot, ash and grit. These create dirt, harm health and reduce visibility. Under certain meteorological conditions, coal burning in London used to create smog – a dense, white fog. This was most likely in winter, when more fuel was burnt and the air was already cooled close to its dew point (the temperature at which water vapour condenses into droplets). Smog formed most readily in anticyclones, when wind speeds were too low to disperse it and clear night skies allowed surface heat to radiate back into space. In high pressure the descending air can create an inversion lid, trapping ground-level pollution. In December 1952 a dense smog lasted without interruption for four days, creating traffic chaos and bringing trade and commerce to a standstill. A subsequent inquiry revealed that an estimated 4000 Londoners had died of respiratory ailments aggravated by the smog.

The 1952 smog led directly to the **Clean Air Acts** of 1956 and 1968. These enabled local authorities to designate smoke control areas, and gave subsidies towards the conversion of appliances to smokeless fuel. In fact, the problem of burning coal would have diminished without legislation, for industries and homes were already converting to oil, gas and electricity. The problem of coal burning is now much

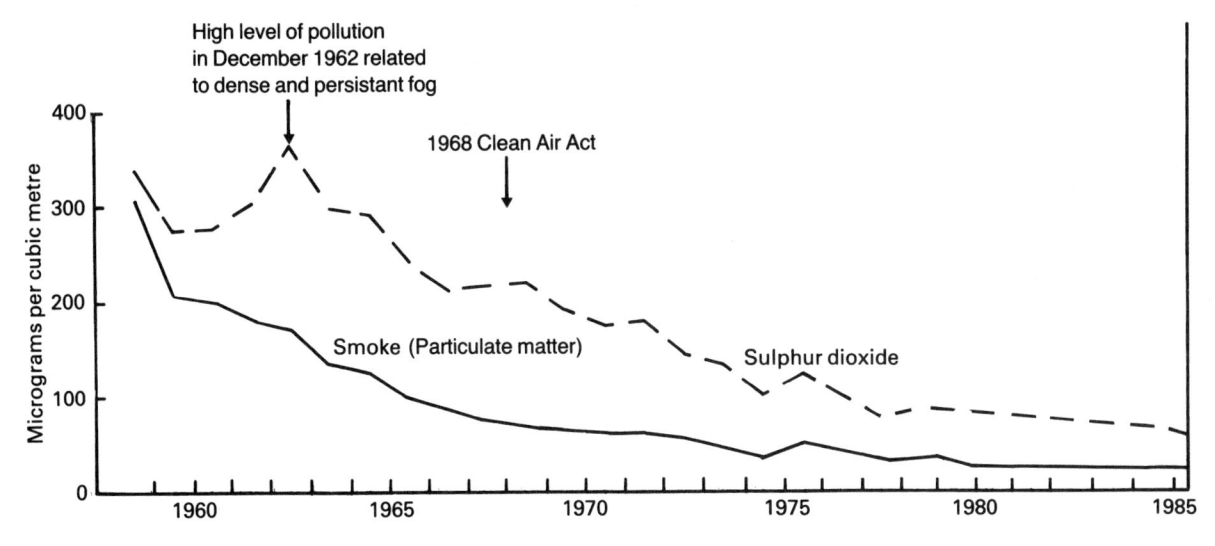

Figure 5.6 Air pollution: winter averages – central London

reduced, and winter sunshine levels have risen by 70% since 1956 (Figure 5.6). The only serious remaining sources of coal-burning pollution are the power stations, who are particularly criticised for the emission of sulphur dioxide. SO_2 may become dilute sulphuric acid in rainwater, damaging building stone and plant life.

The chief source of air pollution in London today is **exhaust from motor vehicles**. Hydrocarbons react with sunlight to produce ozone and this, combined with carbon monoxide, may create a weak **photo-chemical smog**, reducing visibility, attacking metals, plastics and stone, and irritating the eyes, nose and throat. Another dangerous by-product is lead, which is known to affect health and damage the brains of young children. The lead content of petrol is now being brought down by legislation, from a maximum permitted level of 0.84 g/litre in 1971 to 0.4 g/litre in 1981, with a target of no lead by the 1990s.

Noise pollution is also a problem in the city. The **Control of Pollution Act 1974** enabled local authorities to designate **noise abatement zones**, in which they can control noise from premises in specified categories. The government has passed regulations on noise insulation and the internal design of attached houses or flats. Properties close to Heathrow Airport may also obtain grants towards noise insulation.

Revision

1 What are the potential causes of flooding in London?
2 What types of air pollution create the greatest problems in cities?

6

Administering and Planning London

Administering London

While it has always been important to plan London in the context of the broader region of which it is a part, the planning authorities concerned have had little power other than to recommend their views to central government. If these views were accepted, then it was up to the many **local** authorities to implement them, by encouraging or restricting development as appropriate.

The first body with any degree of overall control in London, the **Metropolitan Board of Works**, was created in 1855. The Board set about clearing slums, building roads and constructing sewers, but lacked the resources to achieve any large-scale reform. It was replaced in 1888 by a more vigorous administration, the **London County Council** (Figure 6.1). The LCC became particularly influential after 1919, when it was given the necessary finance to build new houses for the families of those returning from the First World War. The 'Homes fit for Heroes'

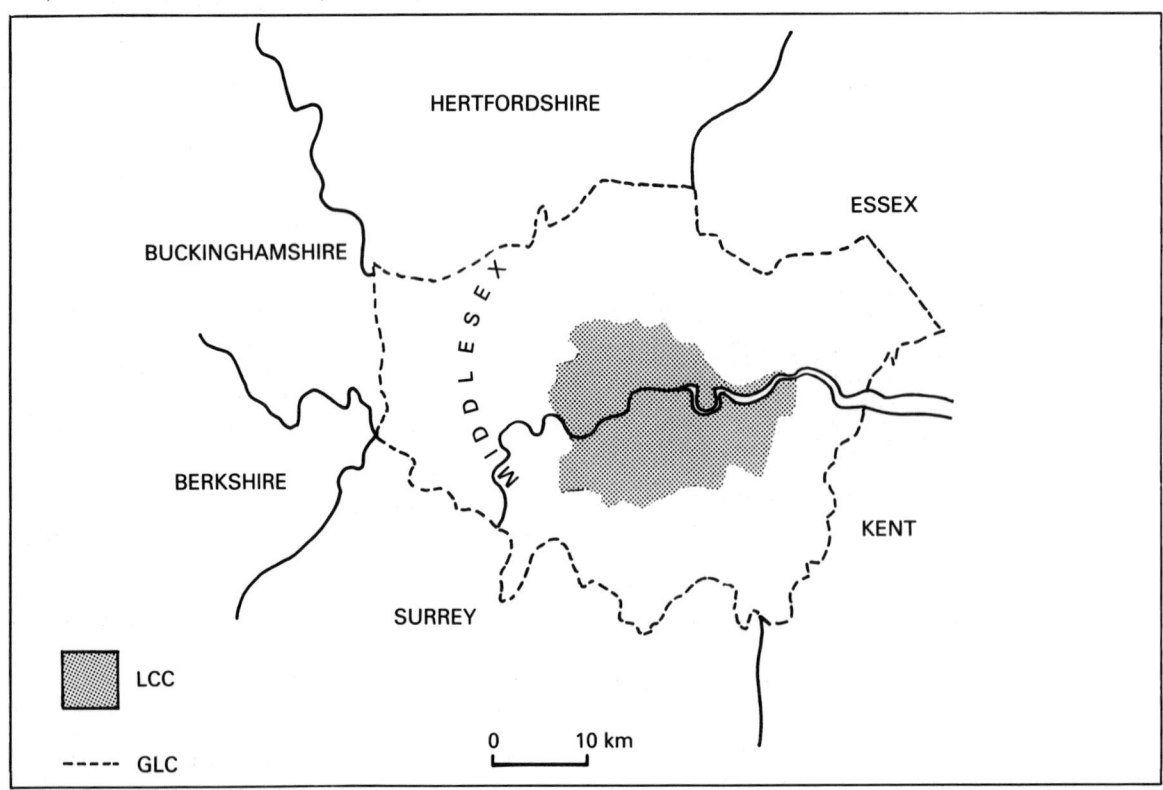

Figure 6.1 Boundaries of the London County Council (1888–1964) and Greater London Council (1964–1986)

policy gave the LCC the chance to develop large housing estates on the edge of London. By 1939, for example, 26,000 houses had been built at Becontree in Essex. After the Second World War, the LCC had the job of rebuilding large parts of London, as well as organising the movement of Londoners to the new towns.

Running a large city required two administrative tiers. One body with overall control was needed, to make decisions about affairs which affect many parts of the city, such as ring-roads, public transport and the education system. Other matters were best dealt with at a local level: street lighting, local drainage and road maintenance, for example. Since the Middle Ages, these local concerns had been dealt with by **parish vestries**. The parishes were both weak and small, and in 1899 were replaced by **municipal boroughs**. As their power grew, the boroughs came to act as a check on the power of the LCC.

Between 1889 and 1964, the built-up area of London spread to well beyond the boundaries of the LCC. Reform of the system was needed, and in 1964 the LCC was replaced by the **Greater London Council**, controlling an area of 610 square miles. In 1985 the GLC was run by 92 elected councillors and a permanent staff of 118,000.

Figure 6.2 Former headquarters of the Greater London Council

The first version of the **Greater London Development Plan** (GLDP) was produced by the GLC in 1969 and finally approved in 1976. It was intended to be a broad **Structure Plan**, laying down general guidelines for the future of London as a whole which would be implemented through the borough **Local Plans**. Since the abolition of the GLC in 1986, the GLDP is being replaced by '**strategic guidance**' issued by the Secretary of State for the Environment to the London boroughs. The boroughs will use these guidelines as the basis for their local plans, to be known as **unitary plans**.

The GLC was also responsible for constructing and maintaining all main roads and traffic management schemes. It ran **London Transport** – the underground network and buses. Through the **Inner London Education Authority** the GLC also managed education in inner areas. It was responsible for some housing schemes, regional parks, refuse disposal, flood control and support for the arts.

The GLC was abolished by the Conservative government in 1986, along with the other metropolitan councils in Britain. By this time it had lost many of its original functions and was seen

Table 6.1 Who manages London in the late 1980s?

Housing	London boroughs
Transport	Buses and tubes: London Regional Transport
	Traffic and roads: Department of Transport and London boroughs
Planning	Joint Planning Commission of the London boroughs, Department of Transport and Department of the Environment
Open spaces and sports centres	London boroughs
Education	Inner London: Inner London Education Authority
	Outer London: London boroughs
Waste disposal	London boroughs, grouped into 8 areas
Water, sewers, flooding, river piers	Thames Water Authority
Fire	London Fire and Civil Defence Authority
Police	Metropolitan Police Authority
Voluntary organisations (grants)	London Borough Grants Unit
South Bank arts complex	Arts Council
Tourism	London Tourist Board
Other	London Residuary Board

as an unnecessary tier of local government. The fact that the GLC was controlled by Labour party councillors, most of whose policies were opposed to those of the government, added a political dimension to the issue of abolition. To the government the GLC appeared to be excessively bureaucratic. Many of the schemes it supported were thought to be a waste of money.

Some of its functions were assumed by central government, others were devolved to the 32 elected **borough councils** and the **City Corporation** (Table 6.1). This Corporation controls the financial heart of the capital. It has the same powers as the borough councils but is of more ancient origin, and elects a Lord Mayor of London annually as the civic head of the City.

Planning the London region: the 1944 Greater London Plan

Until the mid-1960s the basis for planning in London and south-east England was the 1944 Greater London Plan, the work of GLC planner Sir Patrick Abercrombie (Figure 6.3). The plan was based on the premise that London had become unacceptably large. In 1940, the **Barlow Report** on the distribution of industrial popula-

Figure 6.3 1944 Greater London Plan

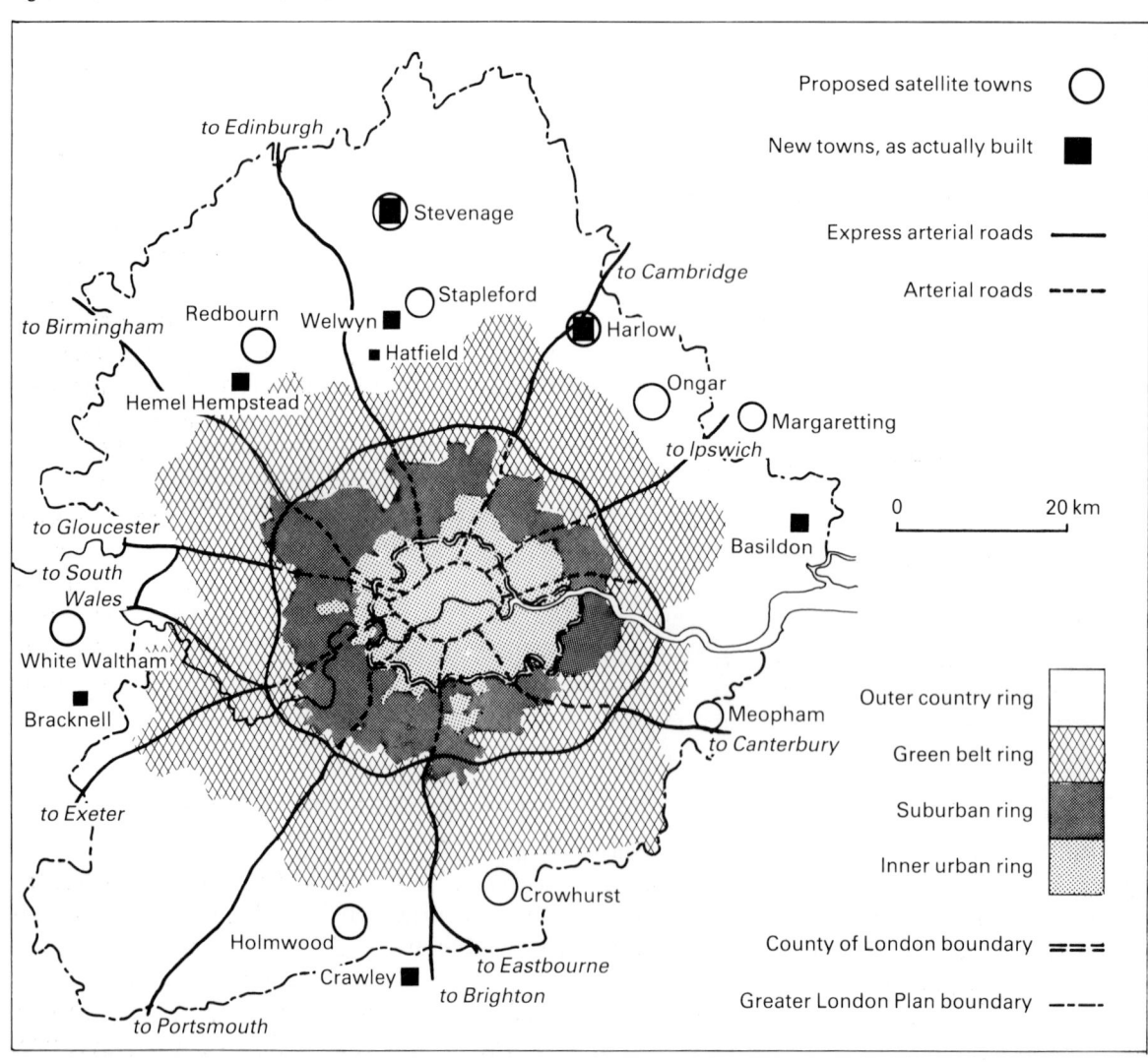

tion had argued that it was wrong to concentrate too many of the nation's jobs in one city. Other parts of Britain suffered unemployment, while London was congested. Abercrombie felt that the only way of dealing with the crowded slum districts of inner London was to move some of the population out of the capital altogether.

Under the plan, eight **new towns** were to be created in a ring not more than 50 kilometres from London. These would draw 380,000 people, as well as jobs, from the capital. This policy was implemented after the passage of the 1946 **New Towns Act**, the eight towns having initial target populations of between 25,000 and 80,000 (Figure 6.3). Existing towns were to expand to take another 535,000 migrating Londoners. The machinery for the creation of these **expanded towns** was set up by the 1952 **Town Development Act**. Twenty-eight settlements became expanded towns, including Ashford, Andover, Banbury and Thetford. The **Green Belt** policy, which had been initiated in 1938 (page 73), was strengthened to prevent further outward growth of London. Development was now controlled in areas up to 50 kilometres from the built-up central area of London.

The plan was based on the assumption that population in the region would not grow to any great extent, that the birth rate would remain at the low levels of inter-war years, and that government regional policy would prevent much migration to the South-East from other regions. Such assumptions proved to be false. The birth rate rose between 1955 and 1964. Migration to the South-East from regions with high unemployment added another half million new residents by 1965. The new towns and expanded towns were insufficient to cope with this growth.

It was nevertheless true that the population of London fell, and the spread of the capital was halted. To what extent this was due to the 1944 Plan is debatable: the problems of London would have produced decentralisation without any government initiative. During the 1960s only one in eight migrants from London actually settled in the planned new towns or expanded towns.

> **Study question**
>
> Why were the new towns around London created?

South-East Study 1961–81

In 1964 the Ministry of Housing and Local Government produced a plan, the South-East Study, to cater for the population growth in the South-East which Abercrombie had failed to anticipate. The new plan aimed to find homes for an extra one million people leaving London, and 2.5m being born in the South-East or migrating to it from other regions, in the period 1961–81. The plan proposed a series of new and expanded towns larger than the original (Mark 1) towns and at a greater distance from the capital (Figure 6.4).

Many of these proposals were eventually rejected because of local opposition, a fall in the birth rate after 1964, and government cuts. Nevertheless, one large new town was started and three major town expansion schemes implemented. The new town was Milton Keynes in Buckinghamshire, designated in 1967. The site already had a population of 40,000, and the plan envisaged adding 210,000 to this by the 1990s. The target figure was reduced in 1977, partly because the problems of inner London were being exacerbated by the loss of people and jobs to the new towns. In the mid-1980s the population of Milton Keynes was 130,000 and it will rise to 150,000 by 1989. The three expanded towns were Swindon, Northampton and Peterborough, all with ambitious target populations.

Strategic Plan for the South-East 1981–2001

In 1970 a new plan for London and the South-East, the Strategic Plan (Figure 6.5), was published by a team of experts from local and central government. The Strategic Plan's main recommendation was to concentrate further growth in the region within a few large centres.

London

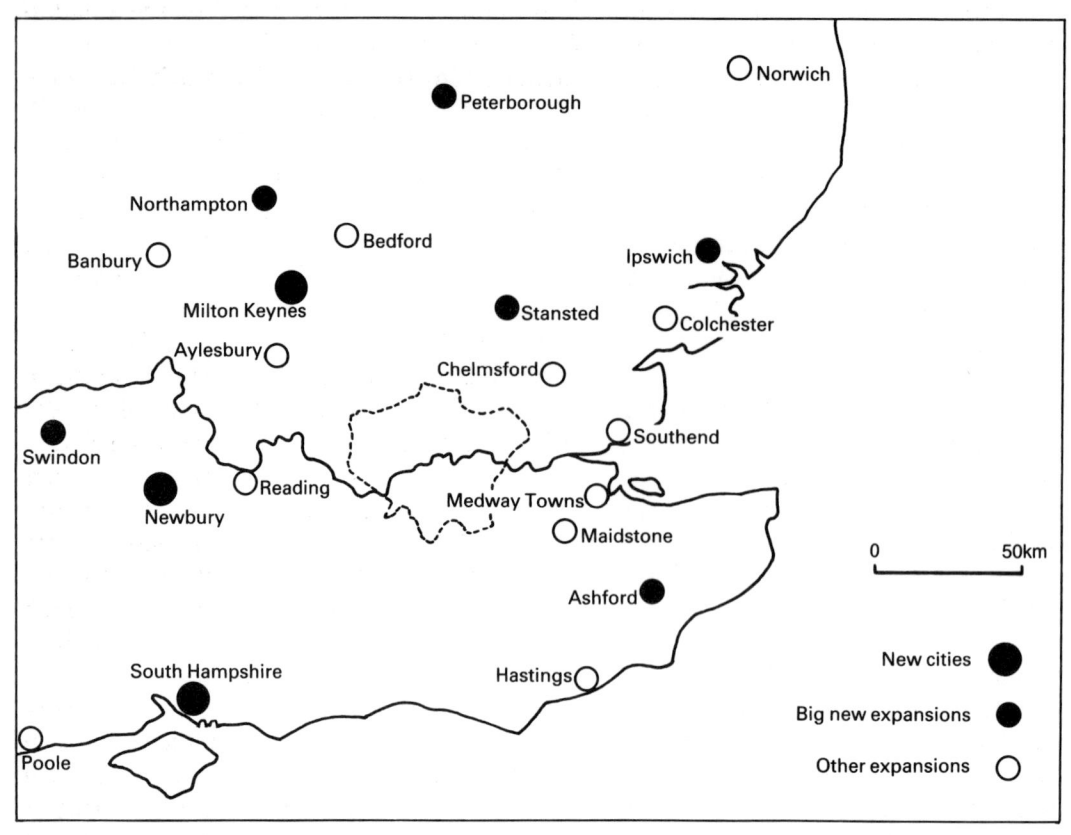

Figure 6.4 South-East Study 1961–81

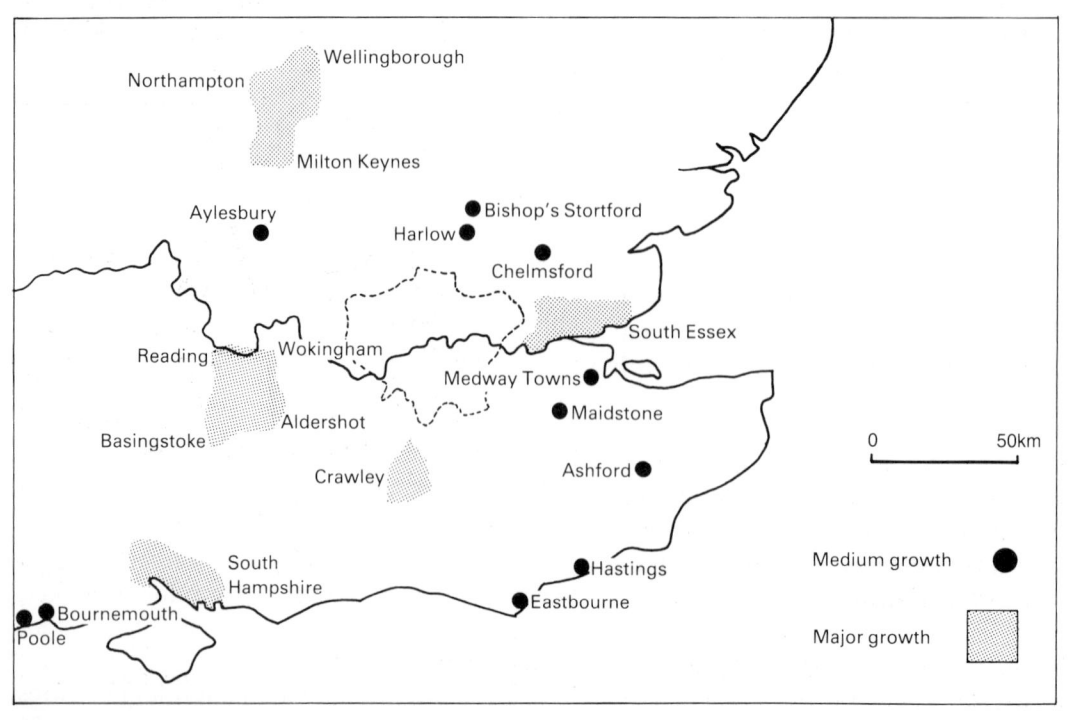

Figure 6.5 Strategic Plan for the South-East 1981–2001

It is cheaper to provide services in larger towns, and industry is better served by larger pools of available labour. Concentrating development would leave more of the countryside unspoilt. Major growth centres were identified as Milton Keynes, Northampton, south Hampshire, Reading, Basingstoke, south Essex and the Crawley area. Other smaller growth centres were also designated at varying distances from London. A review of the Plan in 1978 added the London docklands as an area for growth, in line with policies of inner city rejuvenation.

The South East Planning Council, which had been established in 1965, was abolished in 1979, and since that date there has been no effective overall plan for the London region. With the ending of the Greater London Council in 1986 this problem became even more acute. Local authorities in the South-East co-ordinate their views through the London and South-East Regional Planning Conference (SERPLAN), but this has little power: it merely advises the government. With renewed pressure to build in the Green Belt (Figure 6.6), it may be that a new plan is now needed to specify exactly where development should be encouraged and where it should be restrained. The alternative is a situation in which each local authority makes its own decisions, producing piecemeal and uncoordinated development in the region.

> **Study questions**
>
> 1 Why is a plan needed for a region like London and the south-east of England?
> 2 Why is it so hard to plan more than five years ahead?

The Green Belt

The Green Belt is a zone of land around London within which building development is controlled (Figure 6.6). The Belt is up to 25 km wide and has many towns within it, but these can expand only by infilling spaces between existing housing estates.

The belt was created to stop the sprawl of London and to prevent the coalescence of neighbouring towns. First proposed by the London County Council in 1935, it was given government backing by the 1938 **Green Belt Act**. Some land was purchased by the LCC, but most is still in private hands. The 1947 **Town and Country Planning Act** requires landowners to obtain permission from their local authority if they wish to change the use of any land. With this power, local authorities are able to restrict building in the belt.

The establishment of the Green Belt was a reaction against the huge volume of building in London between the wars. Good farmland was being lost, towns and villages were being caught up in the city's sprawl, and residents of inner London were becoming remote from the countryside. In addition, London was simply becoming too big. Designation of the Green Belt helped to restrict the harmful activities which always seem to grow on the city edge, such as sewage works and refuse dumps.

To some extent, the Green Belt has been very successful. Only about 5–10% of the land which was designated as Green Belt in the 1950s has in fact been built on. In the late 1970s the area of the Green Belt was extended by about 50%, at the request of local planning authorities. A House of Commons Select Committee Report

Figure 6.6 The Green Belt around London

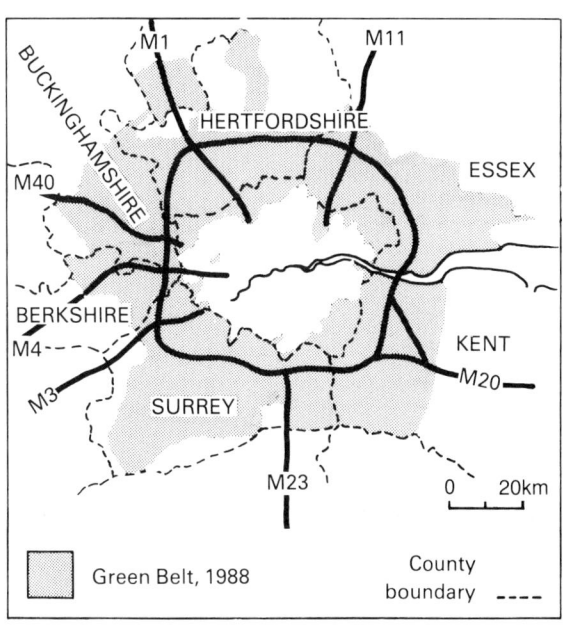

London

in 1984 (**Green Belt and Land for Housing**) confirmed the value of the Belt, and recommended that it should be managed more positively than hitherto.

Although the idea was adopted by most other large cities in Britain, the Green Belt around London has not been without its critics. Planners in the 1930s and 1940s failed to foresee the rate at which London would grow in the 1960s. Migration to the capital from other parts of England, together with a rising birth rate, meant that many more people wanted to live in London. As the city could no longer expand outwards, these people had to look to towns beyond the Green Belt. For many, this meant long journeys commuting into the capital. Some towns within the Green Belt were allowed to expand more than expected. House prices in London have been forced up by the pressure of demand, and densities of new building are also higher as a result.

Today, much of the Green Belt looks rather tatty. To the west of London the impact of gravel workings, motorways, Heathrow Airport, and reservoir construction is all too clear (Figure 6.7). Many farms have been turned over to grazing land for horses. Farmers suffer from trespassers, dumping, theft and pollution. Not enough encouragement has been given to land uses that are acceptable, such as agriculture, and evidence shows that the Belt is used for recreation only by those living on the edge of London.

The construction of the M25 ring-road around London in the 1980s further diminished the sanctity of the Green Belt. Much land has been taken for the road itself, which may act as a magnet for factories, offices and shopping centres. In 1985 a consortium of property developers unveiled a plan to build 12 to 15 new 'villages' in rural areas of the South-East. They claimed that without such developments there would be a shortage of 250,000 new homes in the region by 1990. Some of the proposed town sites, such as Tillingham Hall in Essex, were within the Green Belt. The proposal was rejected in 1987, but the search for new 'village' sites continues.

The future of the Green Belt is to some extent tied up with the problems of unemployment in London. A House of Commons Select Committee Report in 1984 recommended that new developments in the Green Belt should be resisted in an attempt to encourage potential developers to invest in *inner* London instead. In 1985 a group of local authorities in the South-East produced an advisory plan (SERPLAN) which suggested that controls should be particularly strict in the western parts of the Green Belt, in order to encourage firms to look to the east of London, where unemployment is higher.

Figure 6.7 Gravel extraction in the Green Belt west of London

> **Study questions**
>
> 1 What is the relationship between the Green Belt, house prices and unemployment in inner London?
> 2 Who gains and who loses from the designation of Green Belts?

> **Revision**
>
> 1 What are the arguments for and against a London-wide tier of government like the GLC?
> 2 What role have the new towns and expanded towns played in the planning of London?
> 3 Why was the Green Belt created? To what extent has it been a success?

7

Conclusion: inner/outer, east/west contrasts

Since 1978, attention has focused on inner city issues to such an extent that our perception of cities like London is very much one of inner/outer contrasts. Much that is contained in this book may confirm that impression. It is arguable that in the future, however, it is the differences between east and west London which will be seen as being most significant.

Firstly, it is possible to see that contrasts between inner London and the surburbs are diminishing. While unemployment is still highest in inner areas, problems of plant closures and cutbacks are as great in parts of the suburbs and older towns near London, such as Reading and Luton. This is because the most important reason for the decline of manufacturing industry is the relatively poor competitiveness of British goods. It has less to do with whether those goods are made in inner or outer London.

Contrasts in terms of household structure are also being reduced as two parents with children ceases to be the norm: in 1981 one- and two-person households made up 55% of the total in outer London. In terms of socio-economic status, the concept of a poorer inner London surrounded by wealthy suburbs has never been very useful, particularly since the construction of large peripheral council estates after the First World War. Many of the housing problems associated with inner areas can equally be found on estates of system-built housing, or older properties which have not been maintained, in the suburbs.

As described throughout this book, market forces and the actions of governments are combining to change the nature of inner areas: decentralisation from the City, gentrification, the transformation of dockland – these are just some of the ways in which the inner city is showing signs of shedding its image as a uniquely depressed part of the urban fabric.

Contrasts beetweeen London and the semi-rural regions beyond it have been lessening for some years. Any social distinction between the two began to break down once middle-class Londoners moved into rural areas, either for retirement or to commute to the city for work. Even the nature of the agricultural economy has changed as London exerts its influence on the region. As long ago as 1966, Ruth Gasson's survey of farms in Kent and Sussex showed that many were run as 'hobby farms' by commuters or retired Londoners. They bought the farms as a good investment, for prestige, or simply because they were a pleasant place to live. Areas of farmland close to London have been influenced in other ways – by gravel workings, motorways and airports – or have been leased for recreational use such as grazing horses (horsiculture). In these ways the countryside is becoming more 'urban'. Before 1986 one of the most telling contrasts between London and the zone around it was administrative: London had its own extra tier of local government, the GLC. Now that, too, has gone.

Recently, authors have begun to draw on the distinction between east and west London as being the one of more obvious significance. East London has much higher rates of unemployment, more low-paid and unskilled workers, and fewer home owners. These facts have recently been acknowledged by SERPLAN (page 74). As with the inner city, however, the prospects for the eastern side of the capital may improve. The M25 has made the area more accessible, and this process will continue as the

London

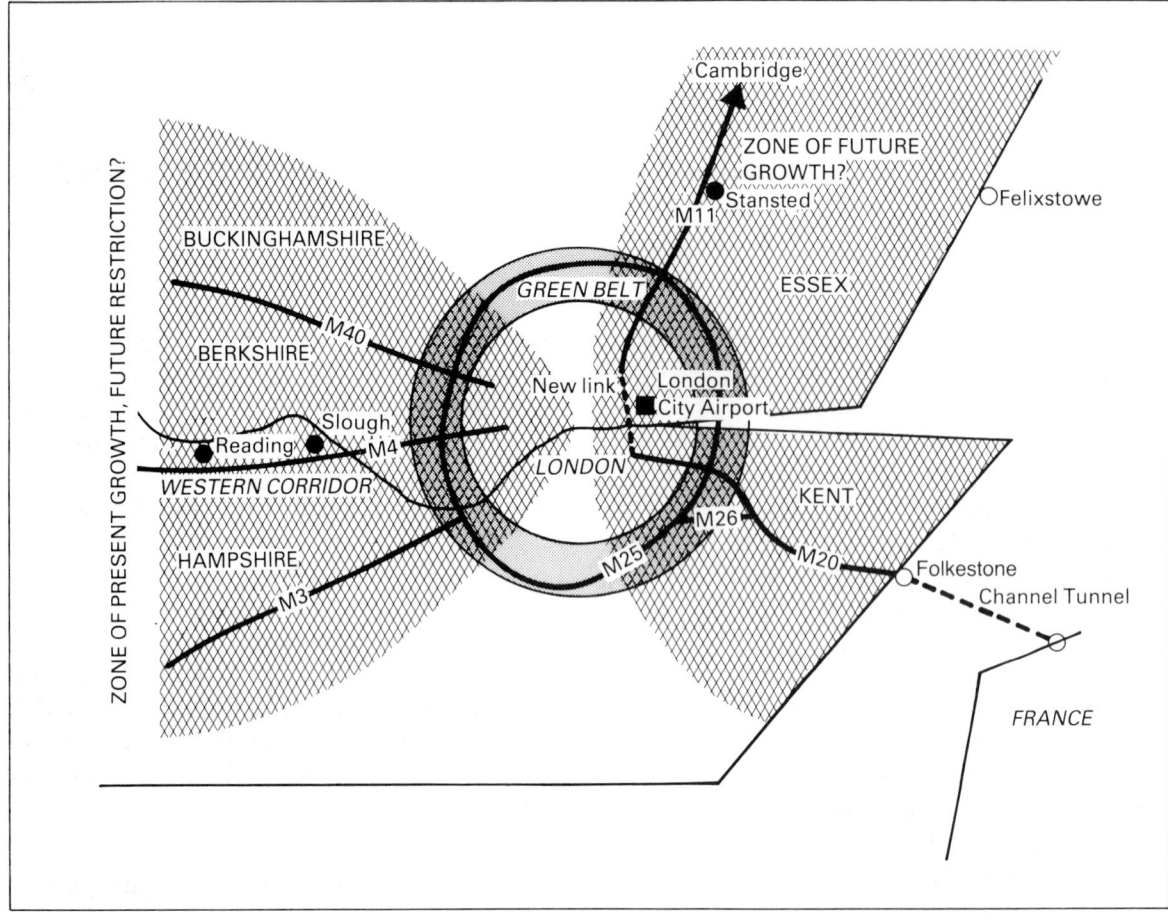

Figure 7.1 London in the context of south-east England

M11 is linked, via a new road through dockland, to the M20. Stansted airport, the London City Airport, a new bridge over the Thames and the Docklands Light Railway will also help to improve the relative position of the east. Outside London, the successful port of Felixstowe and the construction of the Channel Tunnel all add weight to the proposition that it is the east which will gain most from growing trade with the EEC (Figure 7.1). But most significant of all might be restrictions on growth to the west of the city. Berkshire County Council, for example, has already concluded that the county is overcrowded, and is limiting the volume of new house building. Labour shortages are becoming apparent in the Western Corridor. In the battle for investment in future years, it may prove to be the east which has the most to offer.

8

Data sources

This section is to assist those who want to study London further, or do fieldwork in the city.

Libraries

Most local libraries in London hold copies of London census data, although this is of less value if they do not also have maps showing the boundaries of the areas for which the census data were published. Libraries will have local trade directories (such as Kelly's, which can give you lists of local firms back to the nineteenth century), local maps (very useful, especially if you can compare present-day land uses with those in the past), cuttings from local newspapers, and books about the local area.

The best reference library for material on London is the Guildhall Library, off Aldermanbury in the City. This has most of the books written about London, as well as a collection of maps. It is possible to buy copies of old maps here, including Charles Booth's 1899 Social Map of London, which classified roads according to their social status.

Local authorities

The local authority (borough) offices may be able to supply you with a number of useful data sources. They will have copies of the electoral registers for their area – lists of people eligible to vote, recorded house by house, street by street. These are updated every year, so by comparing different years it is possible to examine rates of population turnover (how many people moved into or out of a street in any year). The names of people may tell you something about their ethnic origin. They will also have a list of the rateable value of every building in the borough. If this value is divided by the floor area of the building, it will give you an index of land value. Local authorities may be able to give you details about plans for the area, and some have also published research that they have commissioned on aspects of the borough.

Census data

Most projects use ward-level census data. Each ward has a population of about 4000–12,000. The 1981 census ward-level data is summarised in the OPCS Ward Monitor for Greater London from:

Census Customers Services,
Office of Population Censuses and Surveys (OPCS),
Titchfield,
Fareham,
Hants PO15 5RR
Tel. (0329) 42511

The Ward Monitor gives data on population size, population increase or decrease, population density, sex ratios, age structure, Afro-Caribbean and Asian immigrants, unemployment, housing tenure and car ownership. Maps of ward boundaries may also be obtained from the above address.

The more detailed ward data are more expensive and are sold by the page. The most useful pages from the 1981 Census are:

Page 1 : full breakdown of birth place data
: full breakdown of age structure } 100% data

Page 5 : job structure
: socio-economic groups } 10% sample data
: means of travel to work

Page 6 : further details on socio-economic groups

These data, along with similar data for 1971 and 1961, can be ordered from the above address.

Other useful sources

Goad plans
Plans of larger shopping centres, showing the size and types of shops, can be purchased from:

Chas E Goad Ltd,
Salisbury Square,
Old Hatfield,
Herts AL9 5BR

Maps up to twenty years old may be available, enabling you to examine changes in shopping centres over time.

Parish registers
Some parish churches may be able to give you back-copies of the registers of marriages, births and deaths. This enables you to look at changes in such things as the average age of marriage or death, the occupations of people living in the area, and 'marriage distance' (how far apart a couple were living before they got married).

Books

History of London

P. Adams and E. A. Wrigley (eds), *Towns in Societies: essays in economic history and historical sociology*, Cambridge University Press, 1978
N. Barton, *The Lost Rivers of London*, Phoenix House, 1962
A. Briggs, *Victorian Cities*, Pelican, 1968
H. J. Dyos, *Victorian Suburb: a study of the growth of Camberwell*, Leicester University Press, 1961
E. Ekwall, *Streetnames of the City of London*, Oxford, 1954
C. Hibbert, *London: the biography of a city*, Penguin, 1980
A. A. Jackson, *Semi-detached London*, George Allen and Unwin, 1973
S. Jenkins, *Landlords to London: the story of a capital and its growth*, Constable, 1975
J. R. Kellett, *Railways and Victorian Cities*, Routledge and Kegan Paul, 1969
F. Sheppard, *The Infernal Wen: London 1808–1870*, Secker and Warburg, 1971
G. Stedman Jones, *Outcast London: a study in the relationship between classes in Victorian society*, Penguin, 1981
J. Stow, *A Survey of London, 1598*, Dent, 1956
J. Summerson, *Georgian London*, Penguin, 1962
G. Tindall, *The Fields Beneath*, Temple Smith, 1980
S. Wallman et al., *Living in South London: perspectives on Battersea 1871–1981*, Gower, Farnborough, 1982
G. Weightman and S. Humphries, *The Making of Modern London 1815–1914*, Sidgwick and Jackson, 1983
G. Weightman and S. Humphries, *The Making of Modern London 1914–1939*, Sidgwick and Jackson, 1984

Post-war London

P. Abercrombie, *Greater London Plan 1944*, HMSO, 1945
M. Bateman, *Office Development: a geographical analysis*, Croom Helm, 1985
C. R. Bryant et al., *The City's Countryside*, Longman, 1982
C. Buchanan, *Traffic in Towns*, HMSO, 1963
T. J. Chandler, *The Climate of London*, Hutchinson, 1965
C. Clarke et al. (eds), *Geography and Ethnic Pluralism*, George Allen and Unwin, 1984
H. Clout and P. Wood (eds), *London: problems of change*, Longman, 1986
A. Coleman, *Utopia on Trial*, Hilary Shipman, 1985
P. Congdon, *A map profile of Greater London in 1981*, GLC Statistical Series No. 23, 1983
M. Elliott, *Heartbeat London: the anatomy of a supercity*, Firethorn Press, 1986
English Tourist Board, *Annual Reports*, ETB

L. Esher, *A Broken Wave: the rebuilding of England 1940–1980*, Penguin, 1983
A. Forshaw and T. Bergström, *Markets of London*, Penguin, 1983
R. M. Gasson, 'The influence of urbanisation on farm ownership and practice', Studies in Rural Land Use (7), Wye College
S. Green, *Who Owns London?*, Weidenfeld and Nicolson, 1986
Greater London Council, *Greater London Development Plan*, GLC, 1969
P. Hall, *London 2000*, Faber, 1963
P. Hall, *Great Planning Disasters*, Weidenfeld and Nicolson, 1980
P. Hall, *Urban and Regional Planning*, George Allen and Unwin, 1982
P. Hall, *The World Cities*, Weidenfeld and Nicolson, 1984
P. Harrison, *Inside the Inner City*, Penguin, 1983
D. T. Herbert and D. M. Smith (eds), *Social Problems and the City*, Oxford University Press, 1979
E. Herington, *The Outer City*, Harper and Row, 1984
London Dockland Development Corporation, *Annual Reports*, LDDC
G. Manners et al., *Regional Development in Britain*, 2nd ed., Wiley, 1980
R. J. C. Munton, *London's Green Belt: containment in practice*, Allen and Unwin, 1983
R. E. Pahl, 'Urbs in Rure: the metropolitan fringe in Hertfordshire', (Geographical Paper No. 2), London School of Economics, 1965
Lord Scarman, *The Brixton Disorders 10–12 April 1981*, HMSO, 1981
R. Trench and E. Hillman *London under London: a subterranean guide*, John Murray, 1985
Thames Water, Annual Reports
M. Young and P. Willmott, *Family and Kinship in East London*, Routledge and Kegan Paul, 1957

Acknowledgements

The author and publishers would like to thank the following for permission to use photographs

The Photo Source 3.3a
Topham Picture Library 1.17, 3.3b, 4.5. 5.5
Andrew Wilson 2.4

We would also like to acknowledge that the following figures have been adapted or redrawn from published work.

1.3, 1.4, 1.6, 1.7, 1.8, 1.11, 1.13, 1.14, 2.1, 2.5 from GLC Statistical Series No.23 'A Map Profile of Greater London in 1981' (Figures 48, 36, 49, 5, 1, 63, 60, 62, 31, 20 respectively) by Peter Congdon, 1983

1.2 *Transactions of the Institute of British Geographers*, 1985, 'Integration and Ethnic Spatial Concentration' (Figure 2 on page 368) by David Norman

1.18 *Cities and Towns* by David Burtenshaw, Unwin Hyman Limited

2.8 Advertisement from the Barbican Estate Office as published in *The Economist*

3.4 *Geography*, Vol. 72, Part I, 1987 (page 57) by the author

3.5 Location of Offices Bureau

3.6 *Geography*, Vol. 72, Part I, 1987 (page 58) by the author

3.14 *Area*, Vol. 17, No.2, June 1985 (page 142, Figure 1)

3.17 Southwark Trades Council

3.19 London Docklands Development Corporation

Page 52 and 4.2 *Dockland News*, Canary Wharf Special, No.1, May 1986, London Docklands Development Corporation

4.3 *London under London* (page 152) by R. Trench and E. Hillman, John Murray, 1984.

4.4, 6.4, 6.5 The World Cities (Map 2.3) by Peter Hall, Weidenfeld and Nicolson, 1984, 3rd Edition

4.5 *The Times*, 16 May, 1986

5.1 *Thames Water News*, May 1985, Thames Water Authority

5.2, 5.4 GLC Public Information Leaflet

6.3 *Urban and Regional Planning* (page 99, Figure 26), by Peter Hall, Unwin Hyman Limited, 1982, 2nd Edition

Artwork by Vaughan Collinson

Index

administration   68–70
Afro-Caribbean   15–18
age structure   9–10
air pollution   66–7
airports   60–62
Asians   10, 15–18, 45

banking   30–32
Barbican   27–8
Battersea power station   42–3
Big Bang   35
Billingsgate market   38–40
Blackheath   13
Brent Cross   41
Brixton   14, 17–18
buses   56–7

Camberwell   14
canals   57
census data   77–8
City   7, 30–33, 35–8, 69
City Corporation   70
Clapham   14
Coin Street   34–5
Coleman, A.   22
communications   54–62
comprehensive redevelopment   7, 21–3
conservation areas   33
counterurbanisation   7
Covent Garden   33–4, 38–40
crime   20
Croydon   37

decentralisation   36–41
deck-access housing   21
density   11
Design Disadvantagement Team   22
Designated Districts   19
dockland   12, 47–53
Dockland Light Railway   55–6, 76
drainage   66
Dulwich   13

Educational Priority Areas   18
elderly   8
employment   29–53
Enterprise Zone   50–52
ethnic groups   15–18
Eyre inquiry   61–2

filtering   14
flood barrier   65
flooding   63–5

Gatwick   60–2
General Improvement Areas   22–3
gentrification   14
Goad plans   78
Greater London Council   69–70
Greater London Development Plan   37, 69
Greater London Enterprise Board   47
Greater London Plan 1944   70–71

Green Belt   71–4
Greenwich   13

Hampstead   13
Heathrow   60–62
Highgate   13
hobby farms   75
home improvement grants   14
homelessness   23–4
house prices   24
household structure   8–9
housing 21–8
    problems   21–4
    tenure   25–6
Housing Act 1969   14
Housing Action Areas   22–3

immigrants   15–18
industrial development certificate   46
industry   44–53
inner city   7, 11, 45–53
inner city aid   18–19
Inner Urban Areas Act   18–19
Irish   15
Isle of Dogs   50–52
Islington   14, 20

Jews   15
jobs   29–53

labelling   22
libraries   77
life cycle   9–10
Light Railway   55–6
local authority data   77
Location of Offices Bureau   36–7
London Bridge City   34–6
London City Airport   62
London County Council   33, 68–9
London Docklands Development
    Corporation   36, 48–53, 62
London Regional Transport   56–7

M25   59–60
manufacturing industry   44–53
Maplin   60–1
markets   38–40
MARS   21
motorways   58–60
multiple deprivation   18

newspapers   49–50
new towns   71–3
Nine Elms   38–9
noise   67

offices   30–38
office development permit   36

parish registers   78
Park Royal   46
partnership authorities   19
pedestrianisation   40

pensioners   8–10
plotlanders   44
Plowden Report   18
pollution   66–7
population change   7–8
    density   11
    ethnicity   15–18
    social class   12–14
programme authorities   19
property booms   32–3

railways   54–6
recreation   41–4
rehabilitation   22–3
reservoirs   63
retailing   38–41
Richmond   13
Ringway Plan   58
riots   17–18
roads   57–60
Ronan Point   22
Roskill Commission   60–61
Royal Docks   53

St Katharine Dock   50
Scarman Report   17–18
SERPLAN   73–5
sewers   66
sex ratios   10
shops   40–41
smog   67
socio-economic groups   12–14
South East Study   71–2
Southall   17
Stansted   60–62, 76
Strategic Plan for the South East   71–3
Surrey Docks   50
system building   22–3

Task Forces   19
Thames   57, 63–5
Thames Flood Barrier   65
Thames Water   57, 63–5
Thamesmead   26–7
tourism   41–3
Tower Hamlets   18
transport   54–62
tubes   56–7

underground   56–7
unemployment   29
urban development grant   19
urban programme   18–19, 47

Vietnamese   16
voting patterns   14

water supply   63
waterways   57
West End   12
West Indians   15–18
Westminster   12
wholesale markets   38–40

80